D0906470

Doña Licha's Island

Doña Licha's Island
Modern Colonialism
in Puerto Rico

Alfredo López

South End Press   **Boston, MA**

Copyright © 1987 by Alfredo López

Typesetting, design, and layout by the South End Press collective
Cover by Maggie Block, New York City
Manufactured in the U.S.A.

Library of Congress Cataloging-in-Publication Data

López, Alfredo, 1949-
  Doña Licha's island: modern colonialism in Puerto, Alfredo Lopez.
      p. cm.
    Reprint.
    Bibliography
    ISBN 0-89608-x: $25.00
    ISBN 0-89608-257-1 (pbk.): $9.00
    1. Puerto Rico--History. 2. Nationalism--Puerto Rico-History--20th Century. I. Title.
  F1972.L66 1987
  972.95'053--dc19
                                                                87-15646
                                                                      CIP

South End Press   116 St. Botolph Street   Boston, MA 02115

96 95 94 93 92 91 90 89 88 87   1 2 3 4 5 6 7 8 9

Table of Contents

Foreword

My first book was about Puerto Ricans in the United States and was published in 1973, a year after I finished writing it. I remember being consumed by anxiety, certain that the material would be outdated by the time it reached the readers' hands.

I was 24 years old then and anxiety was my approach to life.

A few months ago, I re-read that book and realized that while I might express some things differently today, most of its analysis remains accurate. The Puerto Rican situation, whether in the United States or in Puerto Rico (this book's topic), basically remains the same.

So, when I explain that this book's publication took over a decade longer than originally anticipated and material contained here was gathered over that period, don't get anxious!

When updating was needed, I did it. When more recent statistical information didn't contradict older information cited, I made no changes. New developments important to the theme were, of course, incorporated.

When I first began working on this book, I envisioned a journalistic study of the impact of colonialism on Puerto Rico—freely tapping the theories, statements, and opinions of knowledgeable people and steering clear of polemics and rhetoric.

I fantasized about people reading it in a couple of nights, getting interested and going on to more scholarly, specific, or definitive material. That kind of a book was needed then and, besides, it was what I felt most comfortable writing. I think the need is still there but I want to clarify some things about the method.

In the text, I use quotes from conversations I have had and interviews conducted over the years. No footnotes are provided for these quotes because there's no source other than my own notes. When I heard things at a public conference, I cited it. I include footnotes to books and articles as an aid to those who want to dig further.

No one invents an idea. Your mind is the constantly evolving product of everyone you've heard, read, and spoken with and every single experience you've observed or lived. So, if you ever took time to speak with me, thanks. I really mean that.

Specifically, I thank my editor, Cynthia Peters, for her outstanding contributions to this book and the entire staff (past and present) at South End. I thank Maritza Arrastia for her informed reading of the initial draft. And thanks deeply to Monica Shannon for her invaluable help with the manuscript because she shared the dream of its publication and because helping others is simply the way she lives.

I dedicated my first book to my father and mother because, by example, they taught me a lot about how to live ethically. I dedicate this book to my sons, Karim and Lucas, because they make it worth living.

And now, while you're reading this, I'll start work on the book I planned five years ago.

Alfredo Lopez
Brooklyn, New York
October 1987

1

Doña Licha

Doña Licha suspected that the devil brought the waves of fish to her island in 1974.

Each day, Licha would stuff a shopping bag with canvas cloth and walk the four winding miles down her hill and up the road to the beach where the palm trees arch stiffly out of the sand and the small stores sell fresh fish and vegetables to the people in cars from the nearby highway.

There she would watch as dawn's light uncovered the water line and the bodies of fish appeared, oily and decomposed from the heat of the water. As the tide receded, more fish appeared. They came up by the thousands that year: black, mouths frozen open, scales covered with oil.

"I thought it was a curse from the devil," Doña Licha laughed, her smooth face opening to show a full mouth of white teeth. "I just stood on the shore with my three children who have families of their own and who all fish with me and we just watched the fish on the sand. It looked like a plague on my life. I cried for days. I thought we were finished. For us, fish are life. I can feel when they are biting. My heart beats faster. It's like some communication with them."

Leticia Roman, Doña Licha, remembers when the people of her area on the outskirts of Ponce, Puerto Rico's southern metropolis, walked to the shores, their pails filled with the day's shining wet catch. "The people would come around noon. We would be back already. We would go out about five o'clock in the morning in our boats, hundreds of boats covering the water like crabs on a beach. That was before the factories came."

When she said these things Doña Licha was sixty years old— an artifact of Puerto Rico's economic past, a fisherwoman who still worked at the trade which had been her family's for centuries and has run in the blood of the people of Ponce since Puerto Rico was a Spanish colony.

"My grandfather owned the largest boat in this town. It was made of wood he himself had cut as a young man. Then, you cut wood at your own risk from the trees, because the Spanish were still here and they took all the good wood to make boats themselves. If they caught you cutting trees they would ride their horses to defecate into your home. They would do worse; killing men and raping women.

"We have black skin. We have slave blood, and even in the early 1800s when my grandfather was still a boy, there was no law against killing a slave blood. Making a boat, if you were black, was a crime. But he made his boat and went to fish.

"I never knew that kind of pain because, when the Americans came here, things became a lot better. I never knew the Spanish, only the American soldiers who would come here to take fish from us."

Licha said these things one day in 1975. As she spoke, she scaled a fish and, without pausing, tossed it naked into a tub of ice, picked up a thick branch with the toes of one foot, and wiped the scales off her thick, sharp knife. The entire process took a half minute. After checking the blade for sharpness and adjusting the kerchief on her head, she began scaling another fish.

"The Americans always wanted the head cut off," she laughed. "It was so stupid. I would scale them well but they were boys who didn't eat much fish." She shook her head. "Such a big country and they know nothing." How much did people pay for the fish? "Two cents, sometimes three. The people paid that," she said looking up briefly. "The Americans didn't pay anything then."

But two or three cents went quite a way back then and, while the fish were plentiful, shimmering in the clear blue waters off the coast of the island, the *pescadores* lived well. Their "industry" was Puerto Rico's most important. "All the islands live from fish," Licha said. "Island, water, fish...obviously."

Those days are gone. "They came with their factories," she said, waving a hand toward the giant petrochemical plants in Guayanilla ten miles away. "They came to commit barbarities on the fish. They made jobs for some but they made the water too hot, the air became thick with the black smoke and the smell, the fish couldn't breathe...they couldn't live in the hot water. Then it started, the waves of fish." Those massive still unexplained deaths were only an anti-climactic symbol of the decline of Ponce's thriving fishing industry. It, like the agriculture of Puerto Rico, had long before succumbed to industrialization; the sudden change thrust upon Licha's island forcibly moved its population, reshaped its economy, and relentlessly attacked its culture.

"At least there are families with men still here. The men could go to work in the factories but my man is dead. I am old and I know nothing else but catching and cleaning fish. What do I know of oil? I thought, how will I live?"

Even though her catch has been cut down to less than a fourth of what it was, yielding her about twelve dollars a day, Doña Licha has learned how to live—she pays no rent, still living in the concrete house her father built about three-quarters of a mile up a hill outside San German, off the road which the military used to make its way around the island long ago. The house is typical of Puerto Rico's architecture, developed to cut material and labor expenses to a minimum. Her living room, the first room one encounters after walking through the always open door, is small with two steel, glassless, shuttered windows looking out onto the road. Licha keeps her color television, her most prized possession, in that room. It's always shiny and on it rest the family pictures and a drawing of the Sacred Heart which she won, two decades ago, in a church raffle. The room includes cheaply made mahogany veneered furniture, with orange patterned material protected by plastic covers. The smell of food drifts in from the kitchen, which is next to the living room, and boasts most of the modern appliances, including stove and refrigerator, but no washing machine—Licha washes her clothes in a large washbasin.

There's a bedroom to the left and to get into it you have to walk through a bead curtain. The bedroom is spartan, except for a large doll with a colorful dress and bandana which stands on a bureau: discreet and proud. It's over thirty years old, made in Spain and given to Licha by her husband as an anniversary gift. Across from the bedroom is the religious room, as Licha calls it: a spare bedroom that has, over the years, become a place of devotion. In the center of the room is a statue of the Blessed Virgin with lighted candles all around it. "I keep them lit because she keeps me going," Licha says.

The statue's appointments are oppulent. An expensive rosary hangs around the Blessed Virgin's neck, holy water in two jars flank her, and a dark velour cloth is her background. It is a typically Catholic display but, for Catholics raised in the United States, the rest of the room would strike a discordant note.

The Virgin Mary has to share her little room with statues from some other religious rites. There is a statue of a black Christ, and of a saint, with horns on his head and a spear, standing over a fallen devil. There are soaps to keep spirits away and little dolls hanging from the ceiling. There are crosses, made out of string, that shoo away the evil curses of others. Licha keeps her voice low, "I want to keep out evil but you don't see here anything that I can use to make evil go to another. I want harm to no one."

Toward the back of the room, in an inconspicuous place almost invisible in the candle light, there is a picture of a young man, still probably a teenager with a shy smile on his face. He wears a U.S. army uniform and has written "to my beloved mother, your blessings are appreciated." The picture is framed in purple cloth. Licha Roman lost her youngest son when the army called him to fight in Korea. She was over forty when he died. "Sometimes I think that it was unfair for him to go. You see it all: they take my fish as they took my son. You ask why I am bitter?"

So each month, Doña Licha walks down the two-mile winding path from her cement home, off the area's main dirt road, to the *bodega* of Silverio Ramirez Acosta. Don Silverio is a creature of habit; the *platanos* he sells must hang from wire hangers the same way, over the same window of his store, all the time. The cans of beans and pigeon peas, which come all the way from the Goya factory in New Jersey, always occupy the same shelves. He himself has been sitting on the same wooden milk crate outside the *bodega* for as long as anyone in the area can remember. And his response to Licha's monthly visit is always the same. He sends his grandson, who helps at the store when not in school, to get his car keys and as Licha approaches, he politely rises, removing the hat from his balding brown head, and offers the keys. "Take my car if you're going to the city," he urges.

"No. It's all right," she protests, "I can walk."

"No, no," he almost shouts, "No woman could walk to Ponce from here. Please, take my car."

After a bit more resistance, Doña Licha nods. She takes the keys and drives the Ford seven miles into Ponce, where she will stand in line with fifty or sixty other people and wait for her food stamps. The lines wind through the government offices, snakes of sweaty, impatient people waiting to buy the key to their survival. A family of four can earn up to 300 dollars in food stamps each month; when there's little to start with, every bit counts. With that money, Leticia Roman can go to the *colmado* (grocery store) in her area and walk along the aisles that are lined with cans and bags of products made in the United States, picking and choosing what she likes.

She buys ten-pound bags of rice, which the store owner helps carry to the car. She purchases twenty cans of different varieties of beans, and meat, sauces, spices, and, finally, an assortment of vegetables. Her purchases fill eight or nine bags, which she piles in the back seat of the car, careful to put the four dozen eggs, shipped that morning from the United States, on top.

When everything is packed away, she skillfully pulls out the food stamps which correspond to the numbers on the adding machine and smiles. The food stamps have done their stuff. "I don't like to take anything from anyone," Licha says, as she leaves the store. "Especially the Americans. They send the food stamps and we eat from them." She shakes her head faintly. "But if it weren't for their factories and that smoke, I would be living from my boat and fish. So I suppose they owe me this." She shrugs. "Anyway, they benefit from the smoke; I benefit from the stamps. We end up even. That's the American way of doing things."

Leticia Roman has lived her entire life on one of the world's most beautiful islands. Twenty-six miles wide across its center, and 100 miles long, Puerto Rico packs into its small territory the beauties typical of virtually every warm climate in the world. In the north, about ten miles outside San Juan, the western metropolitan center which is home to a million of the island's three million people, sits *el Yunque*, a tropical rain forest atop a mountain. There, plants grow to greenhouse perfection and people bask in the sun while being sprinkled by falling rain.

Ten miles south sits the central mountain range, whose land yields the finest coffee beans in the Americas, beans so rich that their fiery red core takes two weeks to turn black, and once black, yields an espresso brew that leaves no aftertaste. In those mountains, there are copper, silver, and nickel deposits which scientists say are among the largest in the American territories.

The mountains are breathtakingly beautiful, covered with evergreen, untouched by the billboards and neon signs that have defaced the metropolitan areas. Sitting atop a mountain in Naranjitas is like viewing a picture postcard of a medieval English summer: the small homes, the cattle, and horses roaming freely, the expanse of grassy plains.

Further south the green suddenly turns into desert, as arid as Nevada's, where one can drive over miles of road without seeing anything but cactus. This is the south of the island, where the industrialization of Puerto Rico started in the 1950s. And yet, two miles away is the sea, and some of the many lovely beaches which gird the island. Those beaches, both north and south, where seventy- to eighty-degree waters come in medium to high waves all day and night, are favorites of champion surfers. At certain points, as in the northern town of Luquillo, the beaches themselves are graced by 100-foot-high palm trees that guard waters ten yards away. At others, as in Pinones, the beach is small and the grass comes up almost to the waterline. At other points, the water meets with large rocks where Puerto Rican reptile life (some species peculiar to the island) thrives and where only intrepid divers leap into the sea.

Smaller satellite islands, Vieques and Culebra, the last of which is considered by scientists to be one of the world's only natural refuges for several forms of prehistoric reptile and animal life, are within a five-minute boat ride of Puerto Rico and, over the centuries, have been considered municipalities of the island government.

This is Licha's island, first inhabited by Indians who were almost all killed off by Spanish "conquerors" in the late fifteenth century. The settlers who came with those conquerors soon brought slaves to work the land, and from these developments came the classes, culture, and economy which shaped the Puerto Rican nationality. Puerto Rico has lived a history in which its own social conditions and development have constantly intertwined with, and been perverted by, colonialism—first as a Spanish colony, then as a colony of the United States. That fact flies in the face of the stereotypes depicted in the magazine ads, the politicians' statements, and the travel brochures. For each quaint example of Spanish architecture, there is a slum born of industrialization; for every breathtakingly beautiful beach, there is an area suffering stultifying pollution; for every example of San Juan's metropolitan glamour, there are hundreds of examples of underdevelopment and squalor

These are the artifacts of colonialism in Puerto Rico. But the perversion is not physical alone. Colonialism perverts the way people look at the world and at themselves; it perverts how they act. Since colonialism and colonies are not static, since nothing in history can stand still in time, the longer Doña Licha's island is a colony, the greater the perversion spreads. The choice for this island is clear: freedom or destruction.

What makes the future of Licha's island difficult to predict is that the future is not in the hands of its people alone. Puerto Rico yields, for U.S. industry, huge profits. Moreover, those economic profits are overshadowed by the political importance that Washington attaches to keeping Puerto Rico from "falling into the camp" of Latin American countries that have declared their independence.

Some people on Licha's island believe the U.S. government would do whatever is necessary to prevent Puerto Rico's independence. There is evidence that in many cases, Washington has already done much. But to understand the present, and to try to perceive the future of this island in the sunny winter of its discontent, it is necessary to understand something of its past.

2

The Beginning

"Rich Port—Friendly People"

Two months after returning to Spain from his first historic visit, Christopher Columbus again set sail for the "new world." Spain was then a merchant power, afflicted with an insatiable plunderer's thirst and, Fernando and Isabella, its rulers, had become intrigued by the birds, the gold, and the Indians brought by the "great explorer" from this "mysterious continent." With the guidance of a group of Indians he had rescued from imprisonment on a neighboring island, Columbus arrived on November 19, 1493 at Licha's island. Today, the date is celebrated as "Puerto Rico Discovery Day" but about the only thing Columbus discovered was that the island was already inhabited.

The residents were called "Tainoes" (although they apparently did not use that name themselves) and estimates of their numbers range from 30,000 to 70,000. On this island which the Tainoes called "Boriquen," they lived what historian Salvador Brau calls "a relatively primitive existence."[1] Unlike their counterparts in Mexico and Peru, the Tainoes kept no records or written history, built no monuments, and constructed no lasting villages. Their economy was based on agriculture and fishing and their society was organized into sixteen tribes led by *caciques*—male chiefs whose power was inherited and who in turn elected a head *cacique* who ruled until his death.

Supported by a network of tribal priests and administrators, the *cacique* ran a society where the division of labor was strict and inflexible. Young men were charged with protecting tribal property and land as well as helping with fishing (for those tribes who lived near the water). The agriculture was, for the most part, in the hands of women and girls who played the traditional role of mothers and housekeepers when they weren't tilling the soil.

Although the land was fertile and farming was relatively easy, Taino life was oppressive, supported by a religion which emphasized the importance of work and the fearsome fate which befell those who disobeyed the tribal rulers. The divine enforcers of that fate, called *cemis*, were worshipped in rites where singing and dancing were performed to the rhythm of the *tambor, guiro,* and *maracas* (the three hand-held instruments of today's Puerto Rican music). In short, as Brau writes: "The society, as in so many cases, was one in which the masses had little say and the rulers had all the power."[2]

And that made Spanish conquest all the easier. Nearly fifteen years after Columbus's visit, the crown sent Juan Ponce de Leon to Puerto Rico with weapons, an army, settlers, and a mandate to rule. The "great colonizer" understood that Spain needed gold to trade on the international market to support its military and its opulent court lifestyle and the only way to get that gold was to convert the Tainoes into miners by winning over the *caciques.* "There will be no problem, your highness," Ponce wrote the king. "These are the friendliest people in the world."[3] So, while subjecting the "friendly Indians" to the brutal work in the mines, the Spanish courted the *caciques* with favors and quickly bought their acquiescence to the exploitation. The *caciques* dutifully told their braves that these Europeans were gods and the braves did not dare defy them. The act of kingly conspiracy and betrayal ushered in the history of colonialism in "Puerto Rico," the name that Ponce de Leon gave this island.

The first two decades of that colonialism were lucrative for the Spanish. "The first smelting yielded 100,000 pesos," writes Kal Wagenheim, "one-fifth was sent to the king: the other four-fifths went to Ponce de Leon and his army and the first Spanish pioneers."[4] But mining proved harder work than agriculture, and it consumed so much of the Indians' time that crops were often left unattended. Disease swept through the Taino tribes as malnutrition, hard work, and the new diseases brought in by the settlers took their toll. To make matters worse, the gold began to run out. Less gold meant fewer favors for the *caciques*, more tension between the Indians and the Spanish, and percolating hostilities which occasionally erupted into war. By the 1520s, the combination of disease, famine, hard work, and war eliminated the Taino workforce. That is not to say that no Tainoes remained—a Spanish census in 1534 counted more than 1000, and probably twice that number had fled to the mountains; but those Indians had escaped work in the mines and were of no use to the Spanish. For all practical purposes, the conquerors of Puerto Rico had exhausted their gold and eliminated their miners.

"The ensuing years were harsh," Wagenheim writes. "Caribes attacked the island town of San German, killing five friars; French pirates called at the same town, sacking and burning it; and the daring Caribes even rowed into San Juan Bay beneath the Spanish cannons and attacked a town on the far shore. The year 1520 was particularly critical. The gold was nearly exhausted and the Indians were almost all gone. Three storms lashed the island and many of the settlers who had bought African slaves on credit were deeply in debt."⁵ As Puerto Rico's economic importance faded, Spain changed its policy and began treating Puerto Rico as a military installation, quickly building fortifications to fend off attacks from pirates and rival countries interested in the "new world." For the next 200 years, the island would mean little economically but much militarily to Spain.

Dark Ages

But that was not the case for all the Spanish in Puerto Rico. Many Spanish settlers had already turned their backs on gold in order to farm the fertile land of their new home. A motley collection of former Spanish prisoners, people fleeing other islands, a few discharged soldiers, and some Spanish "ne'er do wells" seeking a change of luck, they worked the land both for their own subsistence and to produce marketable sugar for domestic consumption. In some cases, these new settlers brought African slaves with them, but the majority brought along, or quickly conceived, their own production team, the family. For the next 200 years, the family would be the island's principal form of productive organization. That, writes Marcia Rivera Quintero, resulted in shared obligations among family members and generally excluded paid work. The work load of the woman was disproportionate...because she worked in agriculture, preparation of food, house care and the birth and caring of children. The house was the center of her activities"[6]

Between 1530 and 1700, Puerto Rico's "Dark Ages," this little Caribbean military base consumed what it produced and tried, with varying degrees of success, to produce what it needed to consume. It was isolated from the world except for attacks by pirates and Spain's European rivals and, although its success in fending off those attacks varied, it survived.

The Puerto Rico of those two centuries barely resembled the highly populated, economically and politically centralized country we know today. A census in the early 1700s found only 100,000 people living on the island and it is probably the case that, at many points during the next 200 years, the population was less than 20,000.

Moreover, it was a population over which the central government in San Juan exercised very little control. To control people, you have to find them. The lush vegetation, mountains, and sweeping plains of the countryside made this more than a little difficult as they formed a kind of "no man's land" to the urbanized leaders. Additionally, Puerto Rico's satellite islands, Culebra and Vieques, afforded the descendants of the Indians a refuge from the vigorous rule of the military government.

In the mountains, among the coffee plants, the *campesino* family toiled, seldom venturing out of its small, parochial terrain, seldom coming into contact with the colonial masters. Its real master was nature—the force that dictated the success of the crops. It was nature at its most ferocious that sent the fires, the droughts, and the storms which forced families to be dependent on one another for survival. It was nature at its most accomodating that protected the family from soldiers and marauders. And it was nature with its dependable rhythms and seasons that developed in the *jibaro* (Puerto Rican peasant) the fierce *campesino* independence and the stubborn resistance to urban life that would continue to show itself into the twentieth century.

In many ways, the *jibaro* was not missed. Most of the trade of the period was in the black market and the piracy the Spanish military was incapable of stopping. And, increasingly, Spain was becoming a shell of its former self. Its European neighbors challenged its supremacy on the waters, England smashed its fleet in 1584, and its subjects in Latin American began challenging its right to rule in their countries.

Domestically, Spain was entering a period of enormous political change. A liberal movement was forming which would eventually seek more constitutionalism at home and a more sophisticated and efficient approach to the colonies. No longer would the *conquistadores'* plunder-the-land-and-let-the-people-do-what-they-will policy be Spain's principal export. All these changes would bring Puerto Rico's Dark Ages to an end and, when it emerged, Puerto Rico would be a nation ready to begin its modern history.

Birth

In 1809, Dr. Ramon Power was on his way from Puerto Rico to Spain to represent the island before the Spanish *cortes*, the parliament constructed principally as a result of Spanish liberal agitation. Facing the great liberal, the island's bishop reminded him that his first duty was to "represent the Puerto Rican people." A century before, the Bishop's declaration would have been scandalous—the very idea of something called "the Puerto Rican people" was unheard of. But, by the beginning of the nineteenth century, the indigenous people of the island had already begun distinguishing themselves from the Spaniards. As Puerto Rico's first historian, Inigo Abbad y Lassera, points out, the Spanish were now considered *el otro bando* (the other group) and Puerto Rico's people were ready to commence what Maldonado Denis calls "the decisive period in our formation as a people, a nation."[7]

A nation springs from a society whose economy, social structure, and culture are developed to the point of distinctiveness—identifiable and accessible to analysis. What spawned the development of Puerto Rico's classes and culture was a series of reforms pushed by the Spanish liberal movement, the movement responsible for getting Power invited to Spain.

Dr. Power went to a Spain where wealthy landowners and businessmen had already wrested much of the essential political power from the crown and the liberal intellectuals had been a major force in that regal divestiture. Yet, while the businessmen sought only to constitutionalize their own country, the liberals also fought for reforms in the colonial possessions. Among the most successful of these liberal efforts were several land reforms, begun in 1730, which aided the development of the sugar industry and also created the island's coffee crop. One typical reform law, proposed in the 1760s by Alejandro O'Reilly—an Irish war veteran sent by Spain to Puerto Rico to survey the situation—called for setting up a sugar mill to make better use of the cane on the island and for relaxing the immigration laws to permit importation of farmers from Spain and other Caribbean islands.

These land reforms were just what was needed by a small group of wealthy landowners, mostly the sons of former Spanish merchants who had made land investments or expatriots from other islands. Logically, the new sugar mill increased the yield from their already lucrative *latifundias*. More sugar meant more money which, in turn, meant the ability to buy slaves and to maintain favor with the Spanish merchants. And as they continued growing, taking over the land of the subsistence farmers, the large landowners also benefited from a more organized system of milling, better irrigation systems, and some control, grudgingly given by the Spanish merchant, over fees.

Through these same reforms, the liberals brought coffee from France which had been banned up until then. The rich landowners quickly took to it since the island's fertile land proved capable of growing a magnificent bean which could compete with any in the world and would eventually prove a highly marketable item. The resulting economy of sugar and coffee defined the classes of Puerto Rican society, classes which would be in almost constant conflict among themselves and against the island's real rulers: the Spanish.

Classes

Colonialism always has one characteristic—its power cuts through the class structure of its colony and, cutting through Puerto Rico's class structure was the dominant group of Spanish rulers, what Lewis calls a "military-administrative-ecclesiastical leadership": a parasitic unholy triumvirate only possible in the aberration of colonial society.[8]

The Spanish administrators oversaw all exporting, and placed heavy taxes on all goods leaving the island. While the merchants were, like their American counterparts, being taxed into a corner, they needed the Spanish army to protect them against pirates and local inhabitants who sought, through occasional revolt and frequent robbery, a more equitable distribution of the wealth. The arrangement of mutual dependence exposed the naked truth of colonialism: that Spain ruled only because it was stronger.

Yet that strength did not always express itself through guns. Spain was, after all, devoutly Catholic and for centuries the church had been an instrument of the crown: willing, as demonstrated during the Inquisition, to use its doctrinaire muscle to discredit and even crush the realm's opponents. From the beginning, clerics accompanied the army under what was an unwritten agreement: in return for the army's protection, the church provided rationales for military and colonial presence. To do that, the clerics wielded an immeasurable cultural power in Puerto Rico. They ran the educational institutions, teaching the Spanish language and a one-God theory, both of which displaced the culture and religion of the African slaves and of the Indians. They decided who went to Spain for further study and discouraged creole youth from doing so.* Indeed, their approach to education was completely political, casting in religious doctrine the Spanish rulers' paranoia about political heresies that could be learned abroad. Even the 1815 reform law, the Cedula de Gracias (which opened Puerto Rican trade to the non-Spanish world), carried a clause prohibiting non-Catholic immigrants from entering the island. The prohibition, Lewis explains, "was based partly upon the fear that religious diversity could only mean stimulating the heresy of political independence," so prominent during that period in the United States.[9] While limiting Puerto Ricans' choice of where to study abroad, the church also limited what they could study at home. The long lists of banned books included Victor Hugo's *Les Miserables*, a book the clerics deemed anti-church and anti-king, and which was banned for a century, and Alejandro Tapia y Rivera's *Biblioteca Historica de Puerto Rico*, which was banned in the nineteenth century because it contained lines of poetry deemed damaging to the *conquistadores'* image.

Creole Classes

The administrators, soldiers, and priests ran the society with Spain's backing, enhancing the interests of the Spanish merchants, but the goods those merchants sold were produced by a society whose complexity rivalled that of Spain, a society of

* The term creole is used to describe people of mixed blood (Spanish and Indian, for example) as well as most island-born people. The Puerto Rican term *criollo* means simply "of the island."

classes with its own internal conflicts. At the top of that creole society were the landowners, the motley mixture which became the island bourgeoisie as a result of the land reforms. They lived in excruciating isolation, resentful of the soldiers, cheated by the merchants, and increasingly afraid of those who worked the land.

Below them were the society's professionals—many the sons and daughters of landowners. Their families' property enabled them to be educated in Europe but they came back only to be treated like dirt by the Spanish, who were seldom their intellectual equals. Disrespected, politically ignored, passed over for teaching and administrative positions, they voiced their anger in speeches, letters, journals, and books published by their Spanish liberal supporters in Madrid. They formed what Lewis calls "a cafe society" and produced a "literature of despair." It's not hard to see why.[10] For these intellectuals took to heart the ridiculous notion that they might someday become worthy of being Spanish citizens (even sharing in Spain's leadership). Had they turned to the rest of the society, those who worked for a living, they would have found people so unfamiliar to them as to be almost alien. These people formed three distinct classes.

Jibaro

Puerto Rican peasants rented small tracts of coffee land from large landowners, barely enough for subsistence. Each year, these *jibaros* would make the trip down the mountains to the towns where they could sell the crops they had not turned over to the landowner. Colonel George Flinter writes of the *jibaro*: "In his straw hat, on his emaciated horse, this unsuitable individual pleasantly moves through the countryside to a mass, dance, or a cock-fight, thinking of himself as the most independent and happy being in existence."[11] The reality was quite different. No one could be more at the mercy of the elements than the *jibaro* family. A fire, a stormy off-season (making the beans unusable), an error in the complicated drying process, or a high wind taking the beans with it could literally wipe out everything the family had. Even when crops did yield harvests, the family was at the mercy of the price-gouging merchants and large landowners, both of whom enjoyed political power the *jibaro* did not have. Yet, Flinter is right in one ironic sense. The *jibaro* was isolated and barely influenced by the colonial rulers.

So, while their daily flirtation with extinction produced a dependence on God—the only thing seemingly capable of controlling these elements—isolation produced a fierce sense of independence, which was strengthened by the family structure of *campesino* culture. In that structure everyone worked the fields (obviously, the more people working the better) and families were extended when possible to include cousins, uncles, and several generations of men and their wives. The women shared the field work and shouldered the additional burdens of the house including the rearing of children. In order to sanctify and preserve these roles, socialization of boys and girls was carried on in separate ways: the boys were raised to become the family leaders and the girls to become what Rivera Quintero calls "little girls with constantly aging bodies."[12]

Yet the independence of the *jibaro* family was combined with a hospitality common to agricultural peoples since access to neighbors' homes ("my house is your house") was often a life and death necessity. A trip though the island on horseback, for example, took days. Where would the *campesino* stay? The mountain winds during a storm were more than capable of blowing a *jibaro* shack off a mountain: where would the family live? And if the crop went bad one year, what would the family do? The combination of individualism and a well defined sense of community formed a central and enduring component of what would become Puerto Rican working-class culture.

Even today the *jibaro* is a folk hero: the subject of songs, poems, graphic art, and an extensive mythology which has often served to cloud an analysis of the period. If there is a Puerto Rican stereotype which characterizes island culture, it is the *jibaro*. And that stereotype is not mere romanticizing; the *jibaro* proved historically resilient, and was the basis for the other laboring class of free people: the *jornaleros*.

Jornalero

Spanish rule would bring few technological innovations to land cultivation; the only way to produce more was to have more people producing. As the coffee and sugar plantations expanded through the 1700s and 1800s, the owners needed more workers and those workers were produced in part by the expansion of coffee plantations which squeezed out the small independent farmers who had until then resisted or escaped becoming tenants of the landowners. Favored by the merchants, richer and better protected (if only by sheer size) against crop failure, the large owner needed only to recruit the services of the Spanish administrators, rearrange some deeds, and kick the small farmer off the land. Administrators cooperated by mandating that all "unlanded" people go to work as day laborers. The *jibaros* who lost their land went, for the most part, to the plains to work in the sugar cane where they joined freed slaves, former soldiers, and "business failures" to form the *jornalero* class.

The *jornalero* was a day laborer, "the agricultural proletariat." The Law of 1849 describes *jornaleros* as "those who have no capital or land," and ordered those people to find acceptable work including "domestic labor," an addition obviously aimed at women.[13] That same law codified brutalization of the worker. The *jornalero* was criminally tried for being unemployed: the penalty was often a jail sentence or physical punishment and a black mark in the daybook, a book which the worker carried at all times. A black mark meant the worker could not get a job, exposing the worker to more punishment. While the law was aimed at bringing workers into the fields, the black book edict served, in part, to repress labor agitation since anyone trying to organize would get a black mark.

Most importantly, perhaps, the labor law concretized the changes that the *jornalero* had brought to the family. No longer was the family a team of production. Women were brought inside to work as cooks and servants. While this was still paid day labor, the fact that there were now landowners who needed many servants harmonized women's daytime work with what they did at night, paving the way for their transformation into full-time unpaid servitude.

The *jornalero* was important to the sugar economy because he or she only had to be paid when work was done; sickness, injury, or any other reasons for not working meant the landowner paid nothing.

Slaves

This was not true of the third class of laboring people sharing the sugar cane fields with the *jornalero*—the African slave. First brought to Puerto Rico in the early 1500s, slaves eventually became the most important source of labor in the sugar industry. While the percentage of slaves among the island population was lower than that of other islands, this is probably because Puerto Rico was agriculturally diversified by the late 1700s and slaves worked principally on sugar. In the sugar-growing areas, their numbers were huge. Ponce, the Spanish census figures show, had a working population which was nearly 80 percent slaves.

By all accounts of the period, the slaves' plight was pitiful. "The whites insult them with impunity," Abbad y Lassera writes. "The rod of the tyrant is always raised and causes disloyalty, desertion, and suicide...they live in poor huts, on a bed of wooden slats which tortures the body rather than resting it."[14] Conditions like those, provoking what Brau says were "countless revolts" by slaves, were not unique, however, for slave-owning societies.[15] What is unique is that in Puerto Rico there was much more intermarriage than in Cuba or Santo Domingo, and this intermarriage resulted, in many parts of the island, in the racial type most often identified as Puerto Rican. In fact, the common anthropological shorthand to describe Puerto Rican culture is that it is a mixture of African and Spanish influences with some Indian impact. There is some truth to that, but it does not tell the whole story.

It is true, for example, that African rhythms drive through the *plena* and the *bomba*, the two principal Puerto Rican folkloric musical forms; and it is true that those forms resemble African communal singing, but the forms had a social importance that gave them sustenance. Historian Migdalia de Jesus de Garcia explains they were the ritualized newspapers of those who could not read. "A chorus would be sung and a principal singer would then take over to tell a recent story about the neighborhood or the landowners." For the illiterate, it was invaluable and far removed from the "literature of despair" that Lewis refers to in his reference to the writing of the island's professional class.

As useful as the term might be, it is potentially confusing to speak of a "Puerto Rican culture." For while there are common threads—language, music, folklore, and customs—they did not suddenly appear and were never static. They emerged from the clash among different classes within Puerto Rican society as it developed and they continued to change and adjust as those classes battled and influenced one another. And, while there was much communality between the emerging cultures of different classes in Puerto Rico, there were also enormous differences. So, for example, while both speak Spanish, the Spanish spoken by an urban professional in nineteenth century Puerto Rico was different in nuance, rhythm, and colloquialisms from the Spanish spoken by a *jornalero*. And that continues to be the case today.

Religious ceremonies among field workers (particularly slaves) often brought together the elements of Catholicism and the religious rites of African pantheism in an attempt to accommodate both the Spanish and nature. The Spanish were aghast at the "pagan rituals...the way the feasts are celebrated, the profane character with which the stations of the cross are viewed...the belief in herbs..." The island's governor, Francisco Del Valle Atiles, called them African religious rites.[16] Slaves knew better than to incur the wrath of the Spanish, so they dutifully practiced Catholicism. But this Catholic faith held few cures for diseases and celebrated feasts in a manner that seemed strange to the more communal Africans. So, when not celebrating Catholic mass, they made communal feasts. When not praying to God in heaven, they treated their sick with herbs.

Slaves also contributed to the graphic arts and crafts of the new society; freed slaves living in the cities had little to sell but their talents as craftspeople. What was once, in Africa, a fundamental skill developed among all people for the creation and molding of artifacts became, in Puerto Rico, a marketable tool necessary for survival. Even today throughout the Caribbean the artists and molders of statues and other artifacts are often black people, practicing inherited skills of tribal societies. Since ceramic arts are one of the most visible artifacts of national culture, the slaves had an enormous impact on Puerto Rican culture. They made the things that would endure.

Finally, Spanish influence can be seen in the selection of staples like rice and poultry, African influence in the form of roasting techniques, and Indian culture represented by food coloring (called *achiote*) which is the same coloring the Indians used to paint their bodies. But contemporary Puerto Rican food is mostly the working-class food of the 1800s, born of the necessity to make cheap dishes from rice, and from the necessity to cook inexpensively by roasting outdoors.

Politics

Not surprisingly, these classes developed a politics revolving around the most significant thing dividing them: their relationship with Spain.

"Puerto Rican society was an authoritarian society," Lewis writes, comparing it to Cuba where, "kings who were constitutional in Spain were absolute in Cuba and ministers who were responsible in Spain could proceed as they pleased in matters affecting Cuba."[17] As Puerto Rico increased in international importance, Spain sought to exercise more control through its colonial government. Ministers, proceeding "as they pleased," proceeded repressively. "At home General Prim had been a leader of the revolution of 1868 against the monarchy," Lewis writes. "As governor of Puerto Rico (in the 1830s), he was a brutal reactionary."[18] Such treatment served to make Spain an ever-present force and an ever-present issue. Three political movements emerged in reaction.

Incondicionales

The conservative *incondicionales* (unconditionals) were strict, sometimes fanatic royalists who believed that Spain was the natural mother whose children should stand behind her during good times and bad. Historian Lidio Cruz Monclova describes them as, "the great warehouse owners and merchants...who dominated the relationship with the exporters of the peninsula and dominated the selling and buying of insular production. [T]heir agents and relations and some land-owners and professionals ...together with them, formed the dominant elements in the colonial economy."[19]

The *incondicionales* sought a return to the protected mercantilism threatened by the opening of the island's ports to other countries. Their logical enemies in this were the liberals—landowners and professionals—who, in pamphlets, books, and printed speeches pushed for open ports and home rule autonomy and engaged the *incondicionales* in acerbic and, at times, explosive exchanges. In the period leading up to the development of the Spanish constitution in 1812 (written in part by Power, who was by then vice-president of the *cortes*), liberal agitation on the island rose to a fever pitch.

The Liberals

While the liberals won the battle in Spain, creating a constitutional republic, Puerto Rican liberals were arrested, deported, or tortured throughout most of the 1800s. And that colonial response is understandable. The liberals advanced ideas such as demo-

cracy, citizenship, and the rights of the citizenry—concepts which
the Spanish government considered unfitting for a subject people.
Yet Puerto Rico's liberals never took the next logical political step,
they never called for independence. Instead, they appealed to
Spain for reforms, becoming as Maldonado Denis writes, "the
most imaginative illusion makers."

While the liberals' pleas for reforms were couched in the poetry
of humanism and the reforms themselves were instrumental in
transforming Puerto Rico and making its economy more efficient,
the liberals did nothing to benefit most people. Except for occasional essays (some of which were, in fact, both impassioned and
articulate), the liberals of the island never took on slavery and
never formulated laws to abolish it, since that, of course, would
have meant economic suicide for the sugar growers who were part
of the financial backbone of the liberal movement. Nor did they
pay much attention to small landowners, subsistence farmers,
and small merchants such as the freed slave craftspeople. Instead,
representation of much of this forgotten population would be
taken up by the period's most important movement—the separa-
tists.

Separatists

Like much of Puerto Rican history, the decade starting in
1860—the period of separatist glory—is shrouded in mystique and
much of it revolves around the great separatist leader, Ramon
Emeterio Betances.

Contemporary writers have fondly recounted that, after returning from medical studies in France, Betances took up the practice
of medicine and, seeing the plight of the poor, was driven to the
nationalism which he would so powerfully articulate. For those
writers, the separatist movement was an army of proud Puerto
Ricans, who threw caution to the wind in seeking the self-
determination of their country, and who finally died in glory at the
hands of the Spanish army.

Reality is, of course, much less romantic. For one thing,
Betances already believed in independence for Puerto Rico when
he returned from his studies. After all, he had studied in a Europe
ablaze with national sentiment that was busy consolidating
republics and toppling monarchs. Besides, there is little evidence
that Betances was driven principally by a desire to help the poor;
his separatist vision reflected a fierce commitment to democracy

as an ideal and a democratic republic, patterned after that of the United States, as a practical goal. Finally, Betances was the leader of a movement of men and women of different interests and philosophies, unified only by the goal of republicanism.

To be sure, he was the movement's most articulate spokesperson, although his passionate writings are rivalled by the essays of Segundo Ruiz Belvis (the liberal converted to separatism, in part because of the latter's commitment to the abolition of slavery). And while Betances was a powerful essayist, no writing surpasses that of Lola Rodriguez de Tio, the author of the original words to "La Boriquena," Puerto Rico's national anthem.

Betances was certainly the movement's principal organizer but, since he was often in exile, people like Matias Bruckman and Mariana Bracetti were left to actually work on the nuts and bolts. Finally, while Betances was the great insurrectionist, Manuel Rojas led the final uprising.

What is important, however, is that Betances's thought captured a historical moment during which the island was ready for self-determination and its colonial ruler was in pitiful state of degeneration. As Betances put it, "There is nothing to hope for from Spain nor from her government. It cannot give us what it doesn't have." And it did not have democracy. A leaflet, undoubtedly written by Betances in 1867, describes what is lacking.

> Not a single son of this country has occupied a post of any distinction...we have been paying immense taxes and still have no roads, railways, telegraph systems and steamships. The rabble of Spain—soldiers and clerks—come to Puerto Rico and squeeze us dry, returning to their homeland with millions belonging to us. The government prohibits schools, newspapers and books. The government insists that the *jibaros* should remain nothing more than lowly day laborers with the *libretas*.[20]

As Betances denounced Spain's treatment of Puerto Rico, he and some of the landowning sectors of the movement were actually driven by a desire to separate from Spain and move even closer to alliance with the United States. This is not surprising. The United States of the time seemed the world's most progressive country—it had recently abolished slavery, reinforced the federal concept and the idea of a constitution, and taken major strides toward the development of a powerful industrial economy. As proof, it stood rigidly and financially behind Latin American freedom fighters. Most of all, while Spain was a degenerate power whose concept of trade was to tax, levy, and gouge every penny it could from the landowner, the United States was an expanding country with plenty of land and potential markets, and a well known sensitivity to overtaxation.

The genius of the insurrectional-separatist leadership lay in its ability to pursue the goal of separatism while appealing to different interests within the movement. This was demonstrated by the insurrectional document, the "Ten Commandments of Man" (adopted in 1867), a masterpiece of accommodation among differing tendencies. It denounced slavery, an attraction for the coffee growers whose rivals, the large sugar growers, thrived on slave labor. It called for free trade and respect for private property, a benefit to all landholders. It called for fundamental democratic rights and elections, a benefit for the intellectuals who would dominate a democracy given their superior knowledge and their finely honed debating techniques. But it did not call for the right to unionize or any other workers' rights; working people, for the most part, were not represented in Betances's movement. Even the slaves who would theoretically benefit most from emancipation stayed away, Maldonado tells us. [21] In part, the slaves probably felt there were not enough of them to make a difference. But it is more likely that the insurrectional movement led by intellectuals and landowners wanted nothing to do with the slaves anyway.

For that matter, the program did not actually call for separation either. Separation, the leaders felt, was a prerequisite to enacting the "Ten Commandments." In liberal hands, the "Ten Commandments" would have been a series of demands on Spain. In insurrectional hands, it was a program to be enacted after Spain was kicked out. And that is what is important about Betances and his movement. As they travelled the island, the insurrectionists might have emphasized different aspects of their program to different revolutionary "clubs" depending on the club's class composition. But these flexible tactics ended when it came to the principle of autonomy from Spain. "Betances was uncompromising in his idea that Spain could grant nothing to Puerto Rico," Maldonado writes. "There should be no negotiations."[22]

The movement's moment for action came in the fall of 1868. Betances was in exile in Santo Domingo hiding from colonial officials and preparing an invasion. According to the plan, his fleet would arrive in Puerto Rico with volunteer soldiers from all over the Americas as revolutionary forces on the island began to establish a republic. As romantic as it seems today, it was an entirely plausible strategy at the time. With a weakened Spanish fleet and the bulk of the Spanish military weeks away, a quick attack would have overwhelmed portions of the Spanish army. Then a more protracted struggle would ensue, and there was every reason to believe that the United States and other American governments would commit their forces to help drive Spain out for good.

But Betances never got that far. A Spanish spy in one of the insurrectionist clubs learned of the plan (kept secret from most members) and informed Spanish officials. Betances and several of his captains were arrested as was one of the chief lieutenants on the island. The latter happened to have with him a list of the major leaders of the movement, and when this was discovered, they were quickly picked up as well. Meanwhile the farmers Manuel Rojas and Matias Bruckman marched on the town of Lares on September 23, 1868 and overtook the garrison there. They declared the Republic of Puerto Rico, raised Mariana Bracetti's flag, and had a priest say a *Te Deum* to consecrate their government. The next day, a few miles north, they were smashed by the Spanish. The concept of "intransigence before the colonizers" was written in both ink and blood and today the "Cry of Lares" is celebrated by independence forces as a holiday.

Comes a Colonizer

Although the liberals kept trying, conditions in Puerto Rico made political reform and economic growth nearly impossible. Reformers were continuously repressed, suffering a major setback as their Spanish counterparts were dealt a near death blow when the Spanish legislature disbanded in 1876, the equivalent of a regal *coup d'etat.* Puerto Rico's economy was continuously subjected to the spasms of international competition. Toward the end of the century, sugar declined in importance as coffee rose, but the daily lives of the Puerto Rican working people never really changed. Even the abolition of slavery in the 1870s did not materially improve the lives of blacks. By 1898, only 21 percent of the total area of the island was under cultivation, and, as Lewis says, "the total amount of money spent on public education, indeed, some twenty thousands of dollars was just equal to the salary of the Spanish governor."[23]

These conditions, along with Spanish intransigence, drove the liberal Eugenio Maria de Hostos to Betances's movement after Lares. The two men travelled extensively, writing, lecturing, and organizing. One of their centers of activity was New York, where a

foco (group) of revolutionaries in exile from Latin America had
formed. The United States was then playing the role which
recently liberated countries play in today's Africa: a refuge and
staging point for continuing the liberation struggles that were to
become an important element in Puerto Rico.

In 1897, a liberal named Apomexedes Mateo Sagasta became
Spain's premier. A short time before, he had worked with Luis
Munoz Rivera (the head of the liberal Union Party) in Puerto Rico
on an agreement granting Puerto Rico home rule. The Sagasta
agreement went into effect when the Spanish liberal took over in
Madrid and was forgotten six months later when the United
States took over the island. The Spanish American War (during
which the United States turned the Spanish out of most parts of
the Caribbean) lasted 115 days but only seventeen of them were
spent in Puerto Rico. Of the more than 16,000 troops that landed,
only four U.S. soldiers were killed and forty wounded in a clean-up
maneuver against Spanish troops, who had already been thrown
out of other Spanish possessions in the Caribbean. The resulting
Treaty of Paris "ceded" Puerto Rico to the United States. The
terseness of the phrase does not convey the potential importance
Puerto Rico had for the United States. Because of its unique geo-
graphical position, Puerto Rico was an ideal Latin American base,
located between Florida and South America, and close to Central
America. It was not, at that point, economically important, but
strategically, it was well worth the seventeen-day skirmish.

In a sense, the people of the island were superfluous when
compared with more important military considerations. There
was virtually no sugar production at this point; the industry had
been killed off by competition. There were only 175 miles of paved
road, giving access only to the northern part of the island. Just 10
percent of the island's youth was in school, 87 percent of the
population was illiterate, 70 percent of the infants died before the
age of six months, and 80 percent of the population of nearly a
million lived in unlighted, wood-thatched huts.

Don Benigno remembers the events:

> Word had already gotten to us that the Americans were com-
> ing. We didn't know much about them but my father told me
> that they would be the color of the Spanish, but more intelli-
> gent. He also told me that they would speak another lan-
> guage. I was a boy of twelve and I had no idea what another
> language was. I just couldn't understand what it meant. But
> things were so bad with the Spanish, they treated us so badly
> that we thought the Americans would be good.

In Puerto Rico they spoke, at that time, of how the Indians thought the Spanish were gods when they arrived. This isn't taught in the schools because my grandchildren don't know it but since we came from the coffee in the middle of the island we are of Indian blood. So this was taught us from generation to generation. Anyway, the people couldn't go to greet them except for one or two of the men who rode on horseback on the only two horses in the area that could make the trip. They returned in two weeks from where the Americans had landed. They told of large ships and sailors, most of them young, who looked at the fort and were amazed at it. They never looked once at the people along the road and our two men said that the people said nothing to them.

News spread as it has always spread in Puerto Rico, by word of mouth. The legislators passed the word on to the merchants of the capital, who lured prospective customers—the wives of the well-off Puerto Rican landowners who were accompanied by their servants—with bits of gossip, jokes, and political news. The wives told their husbands, although the men probably had already heard from their political connections. The servants told the other servants and the masses of land workers who gave the owners their wealth. They in turn told their wives who sent the word through children, or passed the news at washing sessions by the rivers or streams or chatting at a community dinner on Sundays. The priests immediately told their congregations and, slowly, like the tide wetting the sands of the beach, the news spread. Soon, all the island knew: the Spanish, after a 400 year rule, ruled no longer. General Nelson Miles himself tried to assuage any doubts when he landed on the island with his troops. "We have not come to make war upon a people that for centuries has been oppressed but on the contrary to bring you protection..." But, as Wagenheim explains, "Many Puerto Ricans, particularly the autonomists, felt perplexed. They did not, at the moment, feel particularly oppressed. Just seven months before they had won home rule from Spain after years of struggle."[24] The Foraker Act, passed two years after the U.S. invasion, declared that a Puerto Rican governor would be appointed by the United States and the United States began appointing governors in an exercise of political patronage much like the granting of ambassadorships to small and relatively insignificant countries. In the next forty years, fifteen governors would administer the island's affairs. In 1917, all Puerto Ricans were made citizens of the United States in a unilateral action taken by the Congress called the Jones-Shaforth Act. The poet

Carl Sandburg, who landed with U.S. troops on the island, wrote
"Up to then this island had been under the rule of Madrid. Now it
would be ruled by the United States and the people had to feel they
would be better for it."[25] And so U.S. colonialism came to Puerto
Rico.

3

The Man On The Balcony

By 1977, Luis Munoz Marin was an old man. His creation, the Popular Democratic Party of Puerto Rico (PPD), which had run the Puerto Rican government for all but four of the last twenty-eight years, was finally out of office. And so, for the first time in his life, he settled back into inactivity. Cushioned from the tension of daily political life, he could sit in his mansion which overlooked trees, white sands, and mirror-like blue water and, from the vantage point of his fifty years in political life, look down on Puerto Rico as its elder statesman. He could receive political leaders, journalists, and scholars who sought to know more about the recent past and be comfortable that his ideas no longer needed to stand the test of real life. He was playing a role that the elderly frequently play in a world where the young assume the responsibilities.

Still, the role was difficult, partly because the present so profoundly conflicted with what he had predicted. "Today, twenty-five years after the beginning of Operation Bootstrap,"* he said, "it is obvious that...the economy of Puerto Rico and the island's

---

* Operation Bootstrap, the island's massive industrial development program, is explained later in this chapter.

social situation call for real changes."[1] That statement was something of a self-indictment. For no individual Puerto Rican can take more credit or accept more responsibility for what had occurred in Puerto Rico over the last three decades, both the successes and the failures.

Luis Munoz Marin is the father of modern Puerto Rico—a figure whose image transcends that of a mere politician. He is still, years after his death, a "magician" to the people of Licha's island. To them it was not industry that brought factories and jobs, it was Munoz Marin. It was not a new economic order that generalized education, it was Munoz Marin. It was not that new order, and its booming construction industry, that brought housing, nor was it the working people who modernized Puerto Rico. It was that dignified old man on the balcony of his mansion.

Such mystification is logical. Munoz Marin was, after all, the island's first elected Puerto Rican governor, a post he won by bringing to the island a new political methodology combining the populist style of door-to-door, town-to-town campaigning with a platform that changed the way politicians approached and spoke about issues in Puerto Rico. More importantly, however, Munoz was the man who oversaw two decades of the most tumultuous changes in Puerto Rican history, changes which transformed the island's stagnant one-crop economy into a fully industrial one, urbanized its culture, and divided the nation, perhaps irreversibly, by displacing hundreds of thousands of its people.

Under Munoz Marin's leadership, Puerto Rico progressed from a traditional, primitively governed colony to a sophisticated, colonial enterprise where everything—laws, administrative organization, even popularly accepted ideology—works toward the efficient exploitation of the island's natural resources and labor.

But the truth is that, rather than being the work of Munoz Marin, as popular consensus would have it, these developments were the products of the convergence of changes in Puerto Rico's economy and U.S. expansionism, a convergence dramatized by Munoz Marin's political career. From a fiery *independentista*-populist responding to what he perceived as the social problems of his country, he was gradually transformed into a reform-oriented technocrat who became the tool of colonialist planning. Yet, long before his own metamorphosis (and that of Puerto Rican populism), the foundation for the development of modern colonialism in Puerto Rico was already being laid.

The Colony

By 1938, when Munoz's Popular Democratic Party was founded, major changes had already taken place in Puerto Rico, galvanized by three separate developments. First, since the 1920s, the
world economy had boomed as industrialization and rapidly opening markets fed capitalism. World War I, which had realigned
blocks of power, had also rejuvenated the U.S. economy through
armament and supply manufacturing. Second, the demand for
sugar increased dramatically in the United States. As food manufacturers and processors realized its potential as a taste intensi-
fier, sugar became more than something to put in coffee, and the
demand increased far beyond the sugar companies' abilities to
meet it.[2] The war itself also affected sugar demand as war economies always increase the demand for food staples. The third
development was that people switched from smoking cigars to
cigarettes and the cigarette market took off meteorically. There
simply was not enough cheap tobacco to meet the demand.

These three developments sent U.S. corporations in search of
fertile land, and they did not have to look far. Since the U.S.
invasion, Puerto Rican landowners had used their land for
domestically-consumed fruits and some vegetables. Because they
traded very little, they had few international relationships and,
without such contacts, they acquired little capital. Americans who
came to Puerto Rico, on the other hand, had money, trade relations, advanced technologies, and the run of the island.

Puerto Rico was, after all, a territory of the United States run
by a string of governors who treated the job as a paid vacation or a
diplomatic assignment akin to political exile and did absolutely
nothing to protect the island's resources. The island legislature,
created by the Jones-Shaforth Act, was active, but lawmakers had
little power. Indeed, the island legislature asked the U.S. Congress
five times to take up the question of Puerto Rico's status; Washington never even answered the letters. Such a weak legislature could
hardly be expected to pass the kind of restrictions on foreign
ownership, established in some contemporary third world countries, which would have limited U.S. movement onto the island.

Says seventy-three year old Oscar Ocasio,

> There was a time here when fifteen owners administered the
> land. There was work for all the men, many of the younger
> people, and even for some of the women. One could live. But
> slowly the Amalgamated Sugar Company began buying the

land. Acosta, who had 300 acres off the road, all good land, sold it to them. He told his workers, of whom I was one, that during the next month other owners would take over the land. He told us that he would make more profits from the sale than he could make in ten years. He gave each of us two weeks pay and a bottle of rum and said goodbye.

I will never forget Acosta—who was almost six feet tall and towered over each of us by a head, who never smiled at us but, for an older man, could cut better than the best cutters, with his hat in his hand, speaking to us. There were tears in his eyes. Here, he was one of us. I could have hugged him.

I was a young man then, maybe twenty or so, with two children and my wife pregnant again. Since the age of twelve I had worked every day of my life in the cane. My fingers and wrists are still larger than my legs from the machete. I am missing two fingers only. I had learned and was efficient.

The next month was heavy harvest and one Monday all of us gathered before sunrise to sharpen the machetes and go to work.

When we arrived at the fieldhouse for our assignments, we couldn't even get in. We were usually forty or fifty but there must have been two hundred men there. Big men, older and younger men, some who I knew were excellent workers. They had come to get work but I wasn't afraid because I knew my job was waiting for me. Then a tall, well dressed man came out of the house. He smiled and we all felt better. Then he nodded to a teenage boy whom I knew from the area. He was a bully who worked only occasionally but always carried two machetes with him. Their blades were shiny and sharp enough to cut a tree. The man spoke in English, I think, and the bully translated.

The farm had been bought by the company, he said. Higher wages would be paid to everyone. We all laughed when he told us; salaries were almost doubled. But since they were able to do this for us, we had to do something for them. We had to be organized better, so they could make more money. That meant working in something called shifts. I am a man of God and God always makes our shifts. The sun comes up, we work; it goes down, we go to our wives and family. But these men were like Gods. They said some of us would come to work in the afternoon and work four hours, some in the morning, some on Saturdays and, as I bless myself with the cross of the holy Saviour, some on Sunday. Some would haul sugar by lantern off the fields by night.

This was efficient, he said. Some of the work would be done by big machines and some of us would not have to do all the work we once had to do. That was good we thought. But then the devil said we would be paid by the hour. Each of us would work about twenty hours a week. One of us, Gonzalez, a little man who had lost his teeth in a fight with machetes, knew how to count well. We weren't stupid, so we made him count up the hours we would work and the pay we would get. We realized that it was not good pay. And that's how it started.

We would eat fish every night before, now only three nights. Rice and beans all the time. I had to go to the bathroom three or four times a day. Less coffee, not as much bread. The clothes of the children were worn out. We experienced misery. And the bully and his friends became our leaders; foreman they called them. If we stopped work to rest a moment, they would come and spit on us and kick us, beat us with barber straps. If we offered resistance, like one fellow did, they would cut our heads off. A mere child threatening a man...things were turned on their head.

The "efficiency" of which Ocasio spoke—the mechanization of cutting sugar cane, advanced techniques of coffee bean processing, and the superior organization of the workforce in both industries—produced spectacular profits for the American landowners. By the late 1920s, Americans had control of almost all sugar and coffee land, employing 67 percent of the Puerto Rican workers in the two industries, and were routinely making a 100 percent profit.

Like the land reforms two centuries before, these developments profoundly changed the society. The increased need for land workers solidified the agricultural working class as the principal producer of island wealth. There were no longer any slaves and, although there were still great numbers of *jibaros*, most scholars believe that the day laborers had overtaken them in number. In many cases, in fact, *jibaros* worked their own land as a sideline to working for large landowners. And for the first time in many years, women entered the agricultural workforce in enormous numbers.

Labor

While consolidating ownership of the land, these economic changes also consolidated the class that worked the land and the difficulties inherent in organizing different kinds of labor—slaves and free people *campesinos* and land proletariat—disappeared. The ranks of the island's unions swelled with cane and tobacco workers and Puerto Rico's labor movement became as combative, massively organized, and radical as any in the world.

Of course, this labor movement was no overnight creation. Since the turn of the century, labor organizers had already succeeded in forming the Free Federation of Labor which grew spectacularly during the first two decades of the century and the Socialist Party—the first massive, radical working-class party in island history—had been growing steadily since its founding in 1899.

During much of its heyday, the Socialist Party was led by Santiago Iglesias Pantin, a Spanish socialist often referred to as the father of the Puerto Rican labor movement. Yet, while Iglesias's imprint is easily seen on much of organized labor's activities during the first part of this century, evidence indicates that the labor movement in Puerto Rico was more a network of local organizations than the centralized apparatus familiar to most Americans today. And it is additionally clear that this very lack of centralization contributed to the movement's militance and political radicalism. One of the Federation's most important organizers, Luisa Capetillo, has left extensive writing not only on her organizing work but on the radical philosophy she and her comrades advanced. At a time when suffragists in this country were espousing the radical idea that women were the equals of men, Luisa Capetillo organized working men and women, establishing herself as one of the mothers of socialist-feminism.

Like her comrade, anarchist Emma Goldman, Capetillo seized on sexual relations as the symbol of women's slavery. "I had been distributing my pamphlet on free love," she writes of an incident on one trip in which she encountered much resistance to this aspect of her propaganda. "[One woman] was told that the pamphlet was immoral and refused to accept it. I didn't force the issue...but I reject the idea that anything I've said is immoral. I didn't tell any woman to run away with some lover. I only suggested she not be a slave to the one she already has."[3]

Capetillo's inimitable courage won her two distinctions. She was the one sent into unorganized territory while other federation leaders concentrated in areas where the groundwork for their organization already existed. And her job routinely brought her into battle with entire families of the local agricultural class and its lackeys. "No woman would attack a male organizer," she wrote, "but they would attack me. So I had to be prepared to confront not only the women of the prominent families who, having only shortly left agricultural work themselves, were not so weak in a fight, I was also always prepared, and rightly so, to confront men who were so used to beating up women that the idea of chivalry never occurred to them."[4]

Since Luisa was often in the front lines of labor organizing, she took to wearing pants, a second distinction. Old labor leaders of Puerto Rico insist that she was the first Puerto Rican woman to affect such attire, and the fiery, brilliant, and uncompromising "lady of the men's pants" is today a symbol of that tumultuous period in labor history.

The Federation itself soon became the labor arm of the Socialist Party, the party that led labor struggles in the 1920s. Indeed, it was the first party to openly challenge Munoz Rivera's Union Party and to espouse radical thinking. Santiago Iglesias, as secretary-general of the Party, voiced that thinking when, in the 1919 Party Congress, he spoke of the success of the Soviets. "They have eliminated all bourgeois structure," he told the assembled delegates. "They have put Russia on the path that is correct."[5]

Iglesias's comments were issued in a context of strikes, militant confrontation, and a flowering of working-class culture the likes of which Puerto Rico has not known since. There were radical journals and newspapers, two of which were published under the Federation's auspices for over twenty-five years. There were two prominent theater groups, *El Teatro Rojo* (The Red Theater) and *El Teatro Proletario* (The Proletarian Theater) of Caguas. *Justicia*, the Federation's official newspaper, frequently published poetry and short stories alongside its political articles. Alfonso Torres, labor leader Moese Echevarria, and shoemaker Juan Marcano wrote for official publications and in books, apparently published through collected funds. Of these, Marcano was the most powerful writer—a thinker and stylist whose work is relevant even today. While his *Paginas Rojas*, according to Rivera Quintero, is "representative of the worker ideal" of the period, he was also the first writer to clearly and consistently address the issue of women in a manner close to that of contemporary feminists.

Ironically, the men and women who worked in the fields, who performed the menial tasks in small cottage factories, or practiced the crafts inherited from the slaves and Indians created this literature of vitality and dignity as the Puerto Rican capitalist class was dying. The new agricultural order, with the success it brought American owners, killed the national bourgeoisie before it had a chance to play the progressive role its counterparts had played in other countries. This is not to say that no Puerto Rican owned a business. There were, and still are, many islanders who do, some of whom are actually major capitalists. But the cohesiveness of interest, the domination over specific industries (like sugar or coffee), and the clarity of political direction which characterized the landowning class of the 1880s disappeared when landowners were removed from their land by American purchase and take-over. The Puerto Rican bourgeoisie would never rise again.

The new agricultural order did spawn some progressive developments. Roads were laid and the beginnings of an island-wide electrical system were built. Compulsory education was instituted by the 1920s because, as Marcia Rivera Quintero points out, the society had to "make sure workers received the elemental levels of education in order to 'read, write and understand the basic principals of the new institutions'."[6]

Once again, women left the home to work, this time as teachers. Underpaid, overworked, and benefiting only from the most elemental training, thousands of Puerto Rican women went into employment in the schools during the 1920s. There is more than adequate evidence that many went into the fields as well, picking up machetes to cut cane alongside the men. What other explanation is there for Marcano's statement, in 1919: "Women have already been the victims of the tyranny, despotism, and authority of the man and the society. Working class women are our comrades..."[7]

And, for the first time in history, the boss was the colonizer. Until then, landowners had been Puerto Ricans. Now, the land was owned and workers were bossed by people from the colonizing country. These large corporations were absentee landowners and their businesses were attended to by management coordinators, selected for two abilities. As Munoz himself described them: "They understood how to talk to their countrymen and they could communicate with the American companies."[8] That management class would form the technocratic underpinnings of Puerto Rican populism and populism would increasingly reflect the two talents Munoz described.

Like any other manager, this sub-class got its baptism by fire. The 1930s brought a collapse of Puerto Rico's economy. The idea of a sugar boom was based on what Americo Badillo calls "an illusion produced by the artificially high price of sugar on the international market due to World War I demand."[9] At the same time, the southern states of the United States finally caught up in their ability to produce large amounts of cheap, reasonably good tobacco. As Puerto Rico's economic star dove, so did the world economy which collapsed in the late 1920s under the weight of uncontrolled postwar inflation. The island was torn by labor strife. As jobs were being lost, businesses were failing, attempts at cutting salaries abounded, and owners generally tried to tighten their grip on production and costs.

The best known strike was in 1935. Cane workers virtually paralyzed the already problem-ridden industry. Radicalism swept the island, from the socialism which dominated major sections of the labor movement to the nationalism of the Nationalist Party of Puerto Rico which was so threatening to the authorities that, in 1937, 150 police massacred 19 Nationalists and wounded another 100 in an unprovoked attack on a peaceful march. The incident, called the Ponce Massacre, was a stinging reminder of what the government would do in service to its colonial master.

Despite these developments, most politicians of the day were steeped in the traditional approach to politics, oriented solely toward the question of island status and objectively isolated from the island population. The island political parties conducted a debate which Gordon Lewis terms "an almost pathological preoc-cupation...with constitutional status."[10] Those politicians could not understand what Munoz Marin understood: that people were crying out for real change.

Enter the Populists

Luis Munoz Marin was tailor-made for the role he would play—he knew the colonizer and the colonized. As a young man, he had spent time in New York's Greenwich Village working as a writer and satirist and courting the "new thinkers," mainly radi-cals who would eventually become the New Deal's think tank.

At the same time, Munoz was thoroughly steeped in Puerto Rican culture. He had an earthy humor and warmth (reminiscent of the *jibaro*), along with a simple eloquence and charisma. What's more, he had established himself as a patriot. In 1938, while a liberal senator, he announced to the legislature: "What finer goal could we have than our full independence?"[11]

"He came to my town in the late 1940s," Dona Licha re-members.

We weren't used to it and we were sitting in a square in the town, expecting nothing. In those days, the politicians rarely

visited anyone and then it was by car. They would come for a
day and make a big speech.

But he came in a bus covered with banners. One said,
"Bread, freedom and land," and had a *pava* [the hat worn by
jibaros], with the symbol of his new party on it. The other said,
"Give us one vote this year and take it back next year." It was
very *jibaro*, you see. Do us this favor and we'll show you how
good we are...then take it back if we're not. There was no
better slogan for teaching people how elections work.

His bus was equipped with speakers. They played typical
music from our area...*bombas* and *plenas*, with famous singers. And the people came to sit in the square, listening and
singing along. And then from the bus emerged this handsome
man...tall, dignified, with a small moustache and wide smile.
He was not dressed in a suit, but in shirtsleeves. The whole
square stopped breathing.

The local politicians always gave speeches about the
need for this change in status and that one, with quotations
from poets I had never read. But this tall man just walked up
to each group of people and spoke quietly to them. The whole
square was filling up with the music: maybe three hundred
people, but he made no speech. I was sitting with my brothers
and two girls from the neighborhood boats. The man came up
to us.

"Hello," he said, and we greeted him. The men shook his
hand. "I am Luis Munoz Marin and am at your service." We
thanked him and knowing his name as a senator and politician which he already was, braced ourselves for his har-
angue. But he just stood there and after half a minute asked
us how things were going. I find it hard to talk to people like
that, having just met them, but he said nothing and so we
were almost obligated to tell him. So we did.

We told him that the five of us were making the wage that
one person could live on. We told him that all our families
were under one roof. That it was necessary to have weekly
discussions to organize who would use the outhouse, how
much water we would drink, and plan menus. We told him
that we had to cut a quarter of every piece of meat we bought
to cut off the vermin and that we hadn't seen a doctor in six
years. We told him that we trusted no leaders and that
although we said this with respect, if he were a leader, we
would not trust him either. Even if he went to church every
day.

He nodded and nodded. Then he smiled. "You don't know
me and there is no reason to trust those you don't know. But

there is reason to take strangers into your home and feed them and give them food for the rest of their trip to the next home. Give me that food; give me your vote for one four-year term. Let me put my *pava* on and I will solve these problems." Then he told us his plans. There would be factories coming to this area. They would bring work, and the Americans, who had taken so much from us, would have to give back their jobs. This country could one day be free and he would take the first step toward it.

Munoz was a skilled messenger, probably Puerto Rico's most brilliant politician. But, as Licha said, people followed the Popular Democratic Party (PPD) as it split from the Liberal Party in 1938, because it had a program. Summarized in a three-word slogan and cast under the party symbol of the *pava*: "Bread, Freedom, and Land."

It was a slogan that captured the political sentiments of the island's majority. Promising land to people who had been displaced a generation ago was a sure way to capture working-class support. Promising bread to people who were starving would ensure their support. And promising liberty, which could be defined (and would be defined) in various ways, galvanized that support by touching the radical political sentiment on the island. For workers, "freedom" provided a possible connection between the U.S. colonialist system and the system of exploitation on the island. Of course, others—small businesspeople and even the few Puerto Rican landowners—could interpret it as freedom from trade restrictions, high tariffs or, for that matter, U.S. competition. It all depended on which of the many different sectors in the PPD was listening.

And the PPD was a party of many classes and sectors. After his highly publicized split with the Liberal Party, Munoz brought a large section of its radical members with him into the PPD and these populist intellectuals and technocrats formed the ideological leadership of the PPD. They were joined by small urban business owners and some landowners who were disturbed by U.S. treatment of the island but still committed to the concept of reform over revolution. Finally, the base of the PPD was the agricultural working class, won over by the reforms promised in the PPD program.

That working class carried the PPD to victory in the 1940 elections, giving the party a slight majority in the Senate and a mandate to realize its reform program. Laws for minimum wages and protection of workers brought the island into the twentieth century. Laws reorganizing some sections of the government helped eliminate bureaucracy. And then there was the centerpiece of the PPD program—the land reform laws—which set up a Land Authority and gave it the power to buy land, take it over from the government, or confiscate it for tax delinquency, and then offer parcels to workers rent-free—theoretically to insure fuller use of the land.

Of course, it did nothing of the sort. The Land Authority did not dare take over land belonging to U.S. sugar companies; the PPD was not about to take them on at this point. And the land it had was doled out in such small parcels that it was absolutely useless for anything more than building a house. By sending land workers to different sections of the island to take up rent-free residence, the Land Authority effectively served as a kind of population manager for the large land interests. Since most of the plots were near large *latifundias*, the workers ended up living rent-free on their plot and working for the large sugar owners. The law, of course, was spectacularly popular among land workers because it promised a free place to live and some renewed connection with the land, and among large landowners because it gave them labor.

During this reform period, World War II was also being waged and, as a result, Puerto Rico was useful as a military base. Army barracks and training and support facilities had to be built, and the construction boom gave the PPD something else to brag about.

There was only one problem facing the PPD: the reality that Puerto Rico of the 1940s was failing economically even as the United States briskly recovered from economic collapse. There had been no real drop in the unemployment rate, over 30 percent by 1942; economic growth had come to a virtual halt; the construction boom—the product of the war effort—was quickly coming to an end. As noted by historian Charles Hamilton, "The New Dealers and populists knew that almost all their reforms would end up flopping and costing more than they were worth but they were successful because, rather than appeal to common sense, they appeal to obvious needs and concerns. But," adds Hamilton, "the American economy could progress through expansion of its markets, of its influence, and of its military which, after all, spent money and made jobs."[12] Puerto Rico could do no such thing.

In 1941, New Dealer Rexford Tugwell was appointed governor of Puerto Rico and proceeded to make a series of reform suggestions, including land reforms. But he insisted that no reform could take place unless sugar lands were nationalized. Congress did not go for Tugwell's idea, but it still served to earn the ire of the large sugar companies who were aghast that a U.S. colonial governor would call for the nationalization by the colony of a U.S. industry. They lashed out at Tugwell with their pens, tongues, and lobbyists, and since Tugwell was a populist, they lumped him with the PPD as their target. The PPD now had to contend not only with a failing economy, but with a powerful U.S. sugar lobby. To stay in office, it would have to make new alliances to get the economy moving. So Mr. Munoz went to Washington to see his old liberal friends, and during these discussions, between populist and colonialist, the historic compromise which formed modern Puerto Rico was made.

The Compromise

If he was alone in his conclusion, Tugwell was not alone in his analysis of the situation in Puerto Rico. His approach to the island economy reflects the kind of approach common among New Deal thinkers. University of Chicago economist and New Deal analyst Harvey Perloff makes this point in his book *Puerto Rico's Economic Future*, a defense of Operation Bootstrap.[13] In the book, Perloff points out that Puerto Rico had the advantage of a workforce which was out of work because of agriculture's collapse. Such a workforce could be important to the island *and* to the U.S. economy. Perloff also explains the "mutual benefits" plan for the island economy developed by Washington planners in the early 1940s.

First, there would be a preliminary stage of government-owned light industry, a trial balloon to showcase what workers on the island could do, as well as to begin the process of migration to the island's cities. After that, small factories would be sold to U.S. investors who would run them as independent businesses. These businesses, in turn, would bring small needle, packaging, and bottle factories to Puerto Rico—the type of industries which require large numbers of unskilled workers. Then larger industry would be set up to complement the light industry and to recruit from the smaller factories those workers who could be trained and hired to do heavy industrial work.

Just how much the island planners concurred in this three-step process is not clear. By the late 1940s, the Populists spoke of heavy and light industry co-existing in a kind of industrial detente, respectfully sharing the economy. But Washington obviously had plans for continued expansion, and the *Populares*

were facing serious political problems, including an increasingly
angry sugar lobby (which still controlled much Puerto Rican land)
and severe economic stagnation. To stay in power, the PPD had to
get the economy going, lower the unemployment rate, and gain
enough U.S. support to hold off representatives of the sugar industry who were verbally burning Munoz in effigy with increasing
frenzy. The most readily available solution was the program of
increased U.S. investment that Washington was proposing.

The problem for both Washington and San Juan was how to
implement it. If this economic plan was to be put into effect, more
roads had to be built, electricity modernized, and a whole society
put into gear. Most of all, someone had to sell the plan to the
workers who would make it happen and the U.S. businesses who
would invest. Munoz Marin was the ideal man for the job. As he
said: "Obviously, we worked hand in hand with Washington on
everything related to Puerto Rico...what was our alternative?"[14]

To create this new economic system, change had to be made in
the PPD program. "Let's put it this way," Munoz said in one of his
many parables. "You have a neighbor whose support you need and
he agrees to help you. You then say 'I'll help you when you need it,'
no? But what happens if you suddenly move away? The friend will
be displeased and won't help. Well, that is what it was like with our
friends in the United States."[15] No one in Washington was interested, after all, in working with a party which would advocate
independence and so independence (the "freedom" in the PPD
slogan) faded and was finally pushed onto a back burner—
"deferred" as Munoz put it. That was the historic compromise of
Puerto Rican populism, what poet Juan Antonio Corretjer calls
"the covenant of betrayal."

Munoz, of course, would not agree: "The Commonwealth was
autonomous. Of course it needed refinement somewhat, but when
compared with what was before, the total control of colonialism, I
think one can see the tremendous advances."[16] Munoz was right in
one sense: the government structure created by the PPD was the
most advanced form of government that Puerto Rico had ever had.
This advance, however, was not toward self-government, but
toward colonialist efficiency.

As a Commonwealth, the island would be and is now governed
internally by a structure similar to that of the United States. It has
local councils, at the municipal level, which are popularly elected.
It has two island-wide houses of legislation—a House of Representatives and a Senate—also elected every four years by popular
vote. It is run by a governor, popularly elected, who names a

cabinet, usually from one of the two parties—the PPD and the GOP-affiliated New Progressive Party (PPN).

A superficial look at Puerto Rico's political structure creates the immediate impression of scrupulous self-government. Appointed colonial governors are gone. There are no army posts at street corners, no edicts, no evidence of a police state, or the obvious signs of brutal oppression characteristic of classic colonialism. The government oversees an educational system, administers economic structures, designs and maintains roads, develops public policy, and runs agricultural programs. It has a police force and a multi-faceted, even cumbersome, bureaucracy. But the real power over Puerto Rico remains in the hands of the U.S. Congress, which maintains 85 percent of the governmental powers over the island. These powers include citizenship, migration, currency, communications (overseen by the Federal Communications Commission), major laws involving labor relations, and military use of lands (including the presidential power to take over any home on the island during an "emergency"). The United States and only the United States can maintain an army in Puerto Rico and give approval to Puerto Rico's trading with another country. It also controls all the water outside the three-mile limits of Puerto Rico's shores.

The U.S. Congress controls Puerto Rico's destiny. Said Puerto Rican Independence Party President Ruben Berrios in 1977: "The colonial nature of Puerto Rican society is clear when one realizes that, were the Puerto Ricans to vote tomorrow to be independent, it would take an act of the U.S. Congress...to realize that alternative. A country which doesn't have the right to be independent is simply not a free country."[17]

These powers are all incorporated into "Law 600" under the territorial section of the Federal Code and statutes. There is no mention of the PPD's sugar-coated catch phrases—"autonomy," "home rule," or "experiment in self-government and self-motivation"—in that law. Congress was not interested in rhetoric; it was designing the mechanism to sustain colonial power. The new government order ("Law 600") provided a structure capable of building a road system, an electrical system, and a water system to accommodate large industry. It provided the trade and water rights to a business community increasingly upset at paying tariffs for both transport and trade. It provided trade restrictions on the island that made Puerto Rico the kind of captive market businessmen dream of, and it provided a controlled currency which made financial maneuvering and investment that much easier in the pre-computerized banking days of the early 1950s. Finally, since businessmen are always attracted to stability, the U.S. armed forces were on hand.

"This is the man," President Dwight Eisenhower said of Munoz Marin, "who will run Puerto Rico for us. We selected him to be elected."[18] Indeed, Washington viewed Munoz Marin as the individual who would sell the package to the Puerto Rican people. He certainly had the political tools, but he also had opposition and that opposition took its sharpest form in the person of Nationalist leader Pedro Albizu Campos. It was in the confrontation with Albizu Campos that populism showed its fangs.

A Second Cry

There is probably no Puerto Rican more immersed in legend than Pedro Albizu Campos. Today, even those who insist they would never have agreed with him also insist that they knew him, or met him, or were represented by him in court. The few speeches that were recorded can be found in record stores, his articles are collected in books, and his letters are valued museum items.

Such reverence is understandable. Albizu's tall, imposing figure, his quick debater's mind, and his incomparable speaking style were unforgettable in a country accustomed to political mediocrity. His brilliance as a law student at Harvard in the 1920s reportedly translated into brilliance in the courtroom and the ability to handle U.S. law was rare indeed among Puerto Ricans of his day.

But most importantly, Albizu Campos was the most uncompromising and brilliant Puerto Rican liberationist of this century and one of the island's most significant historical figures. And most important among his contributions is something only Betances was capable of doing before him—he accurately identified a pivotal moment in Puerto Rican history as it began to develop and developed a strategy to address that moment. For, if Betances led a movement that addressed the gelling of the Puerto Rican nationality and sought to take that development to its logical extension, Albizu Campos led a Party, the Nationalist Party of Puerto Rico, that was the only force to truly oppose the entrenchment of colonialism in Puerto Rico. Albizu Campos assumed the presidency of the Nationalist Party in 1932, while the organization was still an electoral formation and while American agricultural capitalists were rapidly taking complete control of the productive economy. Perhaps Albizu's thinking is best summarized in a speech in Lares in 1950. "It is not easy to give a speech when our mother is lying in bed and an assasin wants to take her life," he said. "Such is the situation of our country, Puerto Rico."[19]

In hindsight, it is easy to understand how Albizu Campos came to the conclusion about the assassin's knife. Before 1932, Puerto Rican productive land was still largely controlled by local owners; the colonial control over Puerto Rico was political and a political challenge to that control was still possible. But with the destruction of the indigenous bourgeoisie, which had been the most politically and economically stable class in Puerto Rico, Albizu Campos concluded that political challenges were useless.

Much has been made of the passion of Nationalist thinking— Albizu's belief that, since Puerto Rico was autonomous when the United States invaded, the invasion amounts to military occupation thus putting Puerto Rico in a state of war with the United States. And much has been made—not all of it complimentary—of Albizu's insistence on armed struggle as the alternative to that occupation, on the duty of all Puerto Rican citizens to take up arms and on the idea that the "pure" Puerto Rican race was being infected by imperialist germs. This highly selective interpretation of his thinking has made him a venerable but quixotic personality within popular Puerto Rican history.

Unfortunately, many who quote and characterize the man do not seem to have read his writing or his speeches. For the substantial body of written thought he left behind proves that Pedro Albizu Campos was hardly quixotic. He was the first Puerto Rican leader to understand that the changes in Puerto Rico's economy in the 1930s represented the beginning of a decisive colonial entrenchment, and he was virtually the only political leader of the late 1940s to understand that Operation Bootstrap was the finalization of that entrenchment.

Today, more than fifty years after he presented it, this analysis forms the very basis of pro-independence thought, the requisite bottom line for all *independentistas* and most Puerto Rican historians.

The Nationalist Party was not a think tank, however, and Albizu was not an ivory tower intellectual. By his own admission, he was most comfortable speaking to people, and he did that constantly during the early 1930s. He would arrive in a town two days before he was to give a speech and visit with the townspeople. "Everybody knew him because he did cases in the courts," Juan

DeLeon recalls, "and they knew he always won. For our people, the law was a thing we didn't know...only the Americans knew it. He could beat them at their own game and, we all thought, here is a man who could run the government better than they can..."

Albizu Campos assumed the presidency of the newly formed Nationalist Party in 1932, on his return from Harvard. Although the economy faltered and the populist movement was gaining strength, Nationalists were frequently confronted with both an attitude of resignation and a pro-Americanism on the part of many politicians on the island.

A story is often told describing a rally of many island politicians on a lighted stage, decorated with American flags. The Republican Party representative finished his speech and saluted the flag. The stage was set for a man who believed in the "propaganda of the deed," as American lawyer Conrad Lynn, who defended the Nationalists over the years, called it.

Albizu walked onto the stage and under the night lights began removing each little flag and throwing it to the ground. "There was a gasp, which grew louder every time he removed another flag," Juan De Leon, who was a young Nationalist at the time, remembers.

> Who would ever think of taking the flag of this powerful country and throwing it to the ground? But he kept doing it and I remember that the tension was horrible. Half of me wanted him to stop because it was too audacious a move and could backfire, but half wanted him to finish it all. And he did, you see, like he finished everything, like he took everything to its ultimate consequences. He took that large flag and threw it down, breaking the pole in pieces. Then he walked to the front of the stage and began by saying, "American flag, I cannot salute you. I cannot salute the flag of those who imprison my people..." The next day everybody was talking about this courageous young man. The people would say, "He's crazy, but crazy with courage and anger, like the kind of man we need here." Boy, he won followers with that.

To agricultural workers, the small artisans, and small businesspeople, Albizu Campos brought the message that Puerto Rico was occupied and the occupation force was now going to kill the island. Only through armed insurrection, he told them, could Puerto Rico survive.

That revolutionary perspective, also one of the great Nationalist contributions, developed from what poet Juan Antonio Corretjer calls "a mixture of nationalism, mysticism and revolutionary fervor" common among the Irish revolutionaries of the period.[20] During his years at Harvard, a center of support for Irish nationalism, Albizu developed a respect for the Irish Republican movement that would influence him for his entire life. Not only did he constantly evoke that fraternal struggle in his writing and speeches but much of the language used to formulate his theory about Puerto Rico as an "occupied country" is clearly gleaned from the Irish Republican perspective of the day. And, through his support work at Harvard, Albizu Campos widened his perspective; by his own account, he began more clearly to see the links between Puerto Rico and other colonial and underdeveloped countries.

It would seem that such an international perspective, coupled with its sharply focused political-economic analysis of the period, would have won the Nationalists the respect of socialists and communists in Puerto Rico. But just the opposite happened; the Nationalists were left alone, abandoned by the labor movement with its increasing ties to the American Federation of Labor, by the communists with their own ties to the American Communist Party, and by the socialists who were scattered in many other directions, including into Munoz Marin's *Populares*.

Part of the reason, undoubtedly, was that Albizu Campos was not a socialist. He often said that the social system of any country should be decided only after its independence. But the more important reason for this relative political isolation was that the Nationalist Party was a threat to every other political organization. It posed a radical ideological alternative to the collaborationism of the left and the unions and it was singularly militant. The Nationalist Party's involvement with the cane workers in 1935 resulted in some of Albizu Campos's most powerful speeches and articles, thick with descriptions of the workers' plight and analysis linking it with colonialism. His message contrasted greatly with those coming from labor leaders of the period.

Despite that notable involvement, however, the Nationalist Party *was not* a party of agricultural workers. It was comprised principally of small landowners, small businessmen, professionals, and a small percentage of urban workers. The common denominator in this membership seems to be that these were the people forgotten by the reforms put forward by the PPD, and the Nationalists would spend the next fifteen years aggressively recruiting them. During the 1930s, the Nationalists organized *juntas* all over the country and built a massive "cadets" organization of Puerto Rican youth.

The explosive organizing was disrupted in 1937, when Pedro

Albizu Campos was sent to a federal penitentiary in Atlanta, Georgia after an incident in which Nationalists retaliated for a political attack in Ponce by shooting the police chief who had ordered it. Though Campos spent ten years in a U.S. prison, upon his return home in 1947, he proclaimed "I have never been away from Puerto Rico." During the next four years, he more than made his presence felt.

The Confrontation

Others may have been attracted to Munoz Marin's plan for Puerto Rico, but Albizu Campos and the Nationalists were not lulled by the fantasy of progress. From its first public description, they bitterly and actively fought the plan. As he had more than ten years before, *El Maestro*, "the teacher," once again conducted his class in the towns, fields, workhouses, and factories of Puerto Rico.

None of this had gone unnoticed by the PPD and Muñoz Marin. The last thing in the world Muñoz Marin needed was a nationally respected critic of his government. As his own campaigning for Commonwealth status intensified, so did the Nationalist Party's denunciations of him and, suddenly, Munoz Marin found himself under fire, his arguments contradicted by a man as intelligent and forceful as he. The Puerto Rican police intensified their surveillance of Nationalist Party militants. Cars and trucks returning from country meetings were stopped. Albizu Campos himself was under almost constant surveillance, and arrests of Nationalists, mainly on gun-carrying charges, were daily occurrences—an effective harassment for nearly three years. The tension—normal during times of major change—was intensified by the war of nerves between the new government and the Nationalists. The ensuing explosion was no surprise.

One evening in October 1950, in the town of Panuelas, a carload of Nationalists was returning from a town meeting. Two weeks before, their president had revealed that meetings between Munoz and U.S. Secretary of War Robert Jordan had been held during which they discussed ways of stopping the Nationalists and their anti-Commonwealth campaign. Later, in 1953, Jordan himself admitted telling Munoz that if the Nationalists could not be stopped from "sabotaging our mutual interests, then we'd have to get rid of their President."[21] By that, he claimed, he meant arrest for terrorist activity. The story of the Nationalist Party, however, has a somewhat different ending.

Nationalists, their nerves on edge because of constant harassment, needed little provocation to react. The four in a car in Panuelas were no exception. A large police convoy overtook the car and stopped it to search for arms. In the ensuing gunfight, all four Nationalists and two police were killed. The news of the incident at Panuelas spread rapidly. Albizu Campos called on his Nationalists to take up arms and, all over the island, Nationalist *juntas* instructed their members to obey. They fought police for two days in Ponce; only the use of U.S. fighter planes overcame them. Nationalists stormed the police station in San Juan and held siege for six hours. They held the town hall for two days in Mayaguez. And, in the province of Jayuya, Nationalists repeated the action at Lares, taking the mayor's office, replacing the U.S. flag with the Lares flag, and declaring the Second Republic of Puerto Rico.

Pedro Albizu Campos, aging and sick, was held at his house for almost twenty hours while nearly forty police shot at his windows before arresting him and the two other people present—his secretary and one Nationalist comrade. By the end of the uprising, 2000 people were arrested and nearly 200 people had been killed.

The revolt did not end there. In 1952, the Puerto Rican patriots, Griselio Torresola and Oscar Collazo, went to Blair House, the President's temporary residence. The purpose of the trip is unclear—authorities still claim that they were on a mission to avenge the repression of their organization in Puerto Rico by assassinating Harry Truman, but there has never been an admission. Torresola was killed by White House guards, one of whom was in turn killed by Collazo. Collazo's death sentence was commuted by President Eisenhower shortly after and he was freed in 1979, after over twenty-nine years in jail.

In 1954, four Nationalists, led by Lolita Lebron, attacked the Congress of the United States. As the UN approved commonwealth status, the four managed to slip into Congress for their historic protest. They opened their flag, shouted "Viva Puerto Rico Libre," and, while two shot into the air, two shot at Congress itself, superficially wounding two legislators. All four were sentenced to what would amount to life sentences. One of the attackers, Andres Figueroa Cordero, his body racked with cancer, was released in 1977 when doctors gave him four months to live. He went to die in Puerto Rico. The others were released with Collazo in 1980, never once renouncing the acts for which they were imprisoned.

As for Pedro Albizu Campos, he was again jailed for more than ten years, serving time in various prisons and prison hospitals. His legs swelled to three times their normal size as the result of a disease resembling phlebitis. Albizu claimed that, in prison, he had been given radiation treatments which produced this condition. He died in 1964, shortly after his release.

In the end, as accurate as Albizu Campos's analysis was, his party did not lead Puerto Rico to its independence. The reasons for this are many and, as several historians point out, some have to do with the Nationalist program itself. It is clear, in hindsight, that the Nationalists' call for a "citizens' revolution" did not attract the one group of people essential to its success—the new proletariat forming in the island's fledgling industry and increasingly pledging loyalty to the PPD. And the Nationalists, forced to function under almost constant harassment and repression for years, did not have much time for discussing strategy and amending their political program. Indeed, their president was in jail for much of the twenty years that comprise the Nationalists' preeminence.

While it might be easy to criticize the Nationalist program, it is difficult to conceive of a program that might have been more successful. The greatest truth is probably that the Puerto Rico of the Nationalist Party did not massively respond to the Nationalists because most viewed independence as an impossible goal at the time. For the most part, it seems people were ready to follow Munoz Marin and his *Populares*.

This seems particularly true of the island's working class. For example, while the 2000 arrests show that many island people participated in the events of 1950, not one strike was called in support of the Nationalists. The Puerto Rican economy was never threatened by the uprising in spite of the fact that it was the linchpin of American colonialism in Puerto Rico. And though the PPD lacked the commitment to real solutions which formed the ideological center of the Nationalist perspective, the *Populares* could count on the working people that the Nationalists needed so badly.

Loyal Opposition

Working-class support of the PPD was not only a product of that party's program and its vicious repression of Puerto Rican nationalism, but also of the acquiesence of the labor movement, which was by then little more than a loyal opposition. Certainly, that movement could have resisted the PPD and combined with Nationalism to organize resistance to the PPD program. In fact, the PPD's ascendancy showed as much about the state of the labor movement as it did about the true nature of Puerto Rican populism.

The labor movement's flaws had begun to show themselves long before the 1950s. The massive strike by cane workers in 1935 was a wildcat strike, called not at the urging of the Free Federation of Labor but in spite of it. By that time, the Federation was badly split and Luisa Capetillo and her comrade Santiago Iglesias represented not one united ideology but two poles in a tri-partite leadership which, after the 1920s, was unable to function in a unified fashion. Capetillo's anarchism was, perhaps, the most ideologically palatable to the agricultural workers whose culture sported more than vestiges of the rustic individualism of the *jibaro* class. Iglesias, on the other hand, linked himself with the Social Democratic unionism prevalent in the U.S. American Federation of Labor. He soon forget the praise he heaped upon the Soviet Union in 1919 as he took ideological sides with the American socialists who split with the American Communist Party in the early 1920s. The third prong of labor's leadership was the small but vital Communist Party of the island led by people like Vergne Ortiz and Juan Seis Corales.

While it is an attractive analogy, it would be a mistake to view this fragmentation as simply an outgrowth of what was going on in the United States during the 1930s and 40s. For while Capetillo's faction developed ideologically from the culture of the land-workers that was centuries old in Puerto Rico, Iglesias's thinking, and that of his Communist rivals, was a reaction to the rapid capitalization and centralization of Puerto Rican agriculture.

Both the socialists and the communists responded to the pressure of centralized industry with a two-fold strategy. They began relying more heavily on deepening contacts with labor unions in the United States which were, after all, fighting the very same class enemy. The contacts with the AFL became so deep, in fact, that the Puerto Rican Federation became almost a branch of its American counterpart. At the same time, the Federation began signing national contracts (covenants similar to those negotiated by modern day Teamsters) which sought a common denominator of rights, a negotiated bottom line for the workers of entire industries. The logic was that all the owners were from a united capitalist class which seldom, if ever, broke ranks. It was more convenient and politically accurate to negotiate with all of them at once.

While the two-fold strategy seemed logical, it ignored two problems. First, a national covenant, while benefiting many workers, also worked to the detriment of the most exploited sectors of the economy. Cane workers in the southern portion of the island, where the available workforce was largest and production most intense, were earning ten to twelve cents a day for their ten hours; the national covenant's percentage-based wage hikes were ludicrous to them. The Federation's inability to negotiate a minimum wage for cane workers sparked denunciations of the Federation leadership as traitors.

The second problem was more complicated. The capitalist class was American, not Puerto Rican, and the international communist movement had little experience in organizing a colony not controlled by a *national* bourgeoisie. While Puerto Rican workers had class consciousness, as documents and letters of the period clearly show, they also had a ferocious national consciousness, demonstrated by the invitation to Albizu Campos to mediate the 1935 strike.

Historians are divided on Albizu's role and even more divided on why workers, fully conscious of the class composition of his party, invited him to lead a strike. Historians like Rivera Quintero, certainly the island's finest contemporary labor historian, view the invitation as an attempt by the local union leadership to use Albizu's uncompromised militancy to fire the strikers and keep the fires roaring. In effect, some historians imply, the workers' invitation shows more respect for the militancy of the Nationalists than any avowal of pro-independence thinking.

But the question remains: if the workers respected Nationalist militancy, what does that say about their thinking on independence? Would strike leadership seek out a Nationalist if the striking workers did not believe that colonialism was a problem? Strike leadership is, by its very nature, always careful not to take actions which could alienate some of the strikers.

As the photos of Albizu's speeches to workers—and the text of the speeches and articles he wrote—show, cane workers gathered by the thousands to listen to him. A 1934 photo of one of his speeches in Ponce shows workers listening attentively, their numbers filling the square.

The cane workers' strike, which ended shortly after it began, failed simply because, as Rivera Quintero points out, "the workers struck against the very instrument of past strikes [the Federation]."[22] There was no organized support network for the strike; indeed, the Federation was hostile to the strike. But Nationalist intervention, while it could not prevent defeat, reflected a new ingredient in the complex formula of working-class activity—that the status of the island was a political issue the labor movement could no longer ignore. The labor leadership's decision not to support the strike represented a clear departure from the radical, militant traditions that characterized it during the first two decades of this century. Albizu Campos himself put it best: "The union movement and the Socialist Party might have represented a movement of struggle at one point in Puerto Rican history, but at this time [in the 1940s] it became irrelevant...no different than the traitors who seek to entrench colonialism forever."[23]

After the collapse of the Free Federation—partly brought on by the 1934 strike—labor leaders sought to create a new vehicle: the General Workers Federation (CGT). Its perspective on island-wide organizing and its links with various local unions was the same as the Free Federation's and the activities of Socialists within it were the same. But the Socialist Party had ceased to be a power. The Communist Party, which extracted some of the most radical elements in the Socialist Party, had already split from Iglesias's leadership in the 1920s, and what was left of Luisa Capetillo's anarchist tendency had all but disappeared. The anarchists, always somewhat reluctant to accept centralized leadership, had been unable to keep alive the sparks of local labor rebellion which formed the living example of their philosophy. Bitterly opposed to the increasingly centralized, top-down leadership that Iglesias Pantin's faction advocated, the anarchists lost that leadership's resources and found themselves isolated and powerless to do anything against the increasingly centralized capitalism of Puerto Rico.

At the same time, the PPD and its rural reformism attracted workers away from Puerto Rican anarchism and agricultural unionism. Middle-level Socialist leaders flocked to join Munoz's new movement in the 1940s and Iglesias's leadership found itself not only lacking a political base but lacking political organizers.

So the socialists in the CGT were now *Populares*, and when their liberal confreres in the American union movement, wedded to the policies of Franklin D. Roosevelt, seemed so enthusiastic about the new concept of Popular reform, the CGT leaders, from Iglesias on down, gave Munoz their blessing.

The labor movement, possibly the only force which had the social power to put a brake on the PPD's plans, lacked the political mettle and courage of the Nationalists. It blessed Munoz Marin and actually supported the government's repression of the Nationalist Party. For the next twenty years, organized labor would be absent from the political struggle over status.

The Plan in Action

The *Populares'* singular position as the only political movement integrating a perspective on independence with a truly
massive base of popular support helped to install the Commonwealth of Puerto Rico in 1952. It was not completely pro
forma: the U.S. Congress debated Law 600, the legal instrument
which defined the Commonwealth government's limited powers,
for a full two years before passing it. After congressional passage,
the Commonwealth was approved by the Puerto Rican electorate
in a plebiscite in which less than 60 percent of the island's people
voted. The vote was merely a formality. Munoz's cabinet had
already drawn up its plans and much of the legislation creating
agencies for the new development scheme and the plans were
publicly presented a month after the referendum.

With the Commonwealth a reality, the PPD technocrats
began an intense search for industrial investors to put their three-
part plan for economic development, Operation Bootstrap, into
action. They presented, in myriad meetings with U.S. businessmen, their system of business-oriented laws and protections. They
also offered two other important lures, neither of which was written into Law 600. Businesses would be allowed to establish themselves in Puerto Rico and not pay a penny of tax for seventeen
years after which time they would have an option to renew. And
the PPD offered (inherent in this tax policy) the promise that
Puerto Rico would maintain this relationship with the United
States for at least another two decades.

While the land reforms of the early 1940s perpetuated the
PPD's control of the legislature, the promise of an industrial nir-
vana got Munoz elected governor, and the Commonwealth approved. Of course, when stripped of its aura—the political rhetoric
and the magnificent promises—the Commonwealth of Puerto Rico
was designed to make an investor's dream of windfall profits a
reality. And Operation Bootstrap proceeded, more or less, according to plan.

First, concentrating on the introduction of light industry and
the development of the roads, power plants, and water conversion
centers, the new government managed to woo U.S. businesses to
its shores. In 1947, about 100 factories existed in Puerto Rico. By
1960, over 600 factories were operating on the island in what
Dwight Eisenhower called, "the single most impressive plan of
economic development in the free world." The results were impressive: 50,000 jobs were created, unemployment was cut to about 11

percent, and political stability and social progress were evident. By 1955, the number of doctors working in Puerto Rico had increased ten-fold, and six new hospitals had been built. A maze of roads, providing access to every portion of the island, had been paved and the superhighway of Puerto Rico, the *autopista*, had become a modern thoroughfare on which a car could travel the periphery of Puerto Rico in six hours. Hundreds of schools were built and a massive teacher training and education program had begun. "An educated youth," Munoz said, "is the key to the future."[24]

Most impressive of all were the *urbanizaciones*. Four- and five-story buildings (previously unheard of in Puerto Rico) were grouped together in complexes of twenty to thirty. This form of low-income housing soon became the dominant housing model on the island. Migration to urban areas was staggering. In 1945, an estimated 60 percent of the population lived in areas surrounding the cities and in the countryside. By 1955, nearly 70 percent were urban dwellers.

"Massive Changes"

About the massive changes brought on by Operation Bootstrap, Lewis writes, "Industrial revolutions, historically, create new social classes. They mobilize new social energies. They set up new lines of class demarcation. They may brutalize a society because they fail to replace the cultural styles they destroy with healthy new ones, as was the case notoriously with early Victorian England. They may add new impetus to forces that have already commenced the process of community disorganization that has created in Puerto Rico the vast disease of urban restlessness."[25]

Within a decade after the inception of Operation Bootstrap, the agricultural lifestyle of the people, with its extended families, its small parcels of land for growing coffee, fruits, and vegetables, and its custom of living next to families that had been neighbors for centuries was almost completely eliminated for hundreds of thousands of people. In its place was the more frantic pace of a new urban lifestyle tied to a time clock, unfolding in crowded housing projects. The very idea of living in fourteen-story buildings would have been incomprehensible to most island people before Operation Bootstrap; now, it was the predominant way of life for the working class.

Once again large numbers of women worked—this time in the

factories. In fact, during some periods of Operation Bootstrap (when the needle trade was prominent, for instance), women were the only family members working. As the work shifted to heavier industry, women were sent back to the "kitchen."

An essential part of this changed culture was the overhauling of the collective consciousness about political participation. Up to then, politics had been something thrown at people every four years at election time. Participation statistics are poor, but Tumin and Feldman, who conducted the most sweeping personal interviews ever on life and culture in Puerto Rican small towns, believe that before the PPD came to power, electoral participation was an urban affair.[26] Obviously, something changed since over 85 percent of the population, in small towns and rural areas as well as cities, now votes. Puerto Rico became what is popularly considered a democratic country—where people express their opinions in open debate and by exercising their right to vote. The political repression that does take place is only necessary as a supplementary tactic to the fundamental strength of colonialism, which has the support of Puerto Rico's people. While popular consensus is always a flimsy thing, capable of sweeping changes virtually overnight, the fact remains that the commonwealth form of government was entrenched with massive popular support.

All the same, involving such large portions of the Puerto Rican people in the democratic process through the PPD's election campaigns raised expectations about their system and their rights to a level that existed in few other Latin American countries. A Puerto Rican would be more likely to stand up to a police officer, or argue with a government official, after the commonwealth was established. And, while consensus was used to entrench colonialism, the concept of democracy which was part of that consensus laid the basis for potential massive opposition to colonialism. For although Puerto Rican colonialism had become more democratic, it was no more humanitarian.

If anything was evidence of the hardship foisted on the people of Puerto Rico by their government, it was the strategies for population manipulation and removal put together by economic planner Teodoro Moscoso. While the growing industrialization of the economy forced working people into metropolitan centers, Moscoso's studies of Operation Bootstrap's feasibility dramatized a distressing point: although 50,000 factory jobs were created, the shift from agriculture to industry also created 120,000 lay-offs. A safety valve was needed to prevent massive unemployment from disrupting the plan's implementation. Munoz Marin knew that

New York City's garment center could absorb Puerto Rican labor. The government began an intensive campaign to encourage migration to New York. "Whenever you went to the city, you would see these billboards, 'A job waits for you in New York.'" Casildo Detres, who came to the United States during the early 1950s, remembered, "they would offer very cheap rates for the ship ride to this country and told everyone we would find a home here. They set up offices in New York to find jobs in the garment center. They did all that was necessary." The plan unquestionably worked and one of Puerto Rico's economic problems was partially solved through the very undemocratic manipulation of the population."[27]

Between 1950 and 1965, Puerto Ricans came to the United States at the rate of 50,000 a year while only 10,000 returned to Puerto Rico. During the early 1950s, most of those migrating were men who would come to New York City and then send for their families. At this time in Puerto Rico, the dominant feature of the economy was light industry which mainly employed women. The preponderance of women in the Puerto Rican workforce caused certain social problems—the solutions to which were even more Machiavellian than the government's emigration policy. When it was clear, for example that large numbers of women entering the workforce were having problems finding daycare facilities for their children, the government began procedures of forced sterilization.

Sterilization, usually the cutting of the fallopian tubes, is an irreversible surgical procedure which renders a woman incapable of conceiving children. Says Doctor Helen Rodriguez, a pediatrician and Puerto Rican activist: "It is a horrible experience. The trauma, the psychological impact is rivalled only by the medical complications possible. Most of all, the operation is irreversible. You can remove an IUD but you can't re-tie the tubes."[28] In 1945, 34 percent of all Puerto Rican women of childbearing age were sterilized, two-thirds of them between eighteen and twenty-four years of age. The percentage has continued to this day. The numbers are startling but easily understandable. "The lack of family support services, of legal and safe abortions, of alternative methods of contraception and of full information about the permanency of sterilization have all combined to produce those startling numbers," Dr. Rodriguez says. "Freedom of choice requires real alternatives."[29] Obviously, there were no alternatives. The jaded sexism of the "Bootstrap" planners meshed with what seems, in hindsight, to have been an almost fanatical determination to bring industrialization to the island. Not only did babies get in the way of women going to work, a process which was essential for the first developmental stage of Operation Bootstrap, but they were a burden to the system; they had to eat, to be schooled, and eventually, to be housed.

Moscoso looked at population figures and discovered, as U.S. economist William Kelly said, "There existed in Puerto Rico a severe problem of over-population."[30] "Over-population" meant that there was not enough food to go around. Puerto Rico's Operation Bootstrap could not feed its people and, as that became obvious to Moscoso and Muñoz Marin, they sought to make the economy more effective by shrinking the population. In fact, in 1973, then Governor Rafael Hernandez Colon announced a new government policy which he hoped would move the country closer to zero population growth: free sterilization to any Puerto Rican woman who wanted it. Supported by federal funds, sterilization was the only free medical service offered to Puerto Rican women. It was a service most often made available right after childbirth when they were still suffering the effects of anesthesia and the "trauma" of an untrained delivery. The rationale was that sterilization was easier surgically at that point, but in reality it was easier to get women to sign papers for the operation.

For those who were not pregnant, the government put together a massive literature campaign about *la operacion*, replete with warnings about starving children, the dire dangers of childbirth, and the pain which accompanies an unnatural birth by surgical cutting. This propaganda has been supported by federal money for the last thirty years and constitutes the longest running successful "informational campaign" by the Puerto Rican government in the island's history. Kelley estimates that the "success of the sterilization control measure" prevented two births every day.[31]

These were Operation Bootstrap's "enabling" programs, responsible not only for uprooting hundreds of thousands of poor people, forcing them to become refugees, but also for the wholesale mutilation of women's bodies. These undemocratic and inhuman procedures enacted by Operation Bootstrap (to compensate for its failures) are evidence enough that the economic program was a failure.

Cracks In The Seams

Operation Bootstrap was to have brought both light and heavy industry to Puerto Rico to co-exist in a kind of industrial *detente* which would simultaneously employ large numbers of people in the heavy industries and give Puerto Ricans a chance to go into business themselves in some of the lighter industries. By 1965, however, the seams had split open and the problems inherent in the plan were revealed.

First, while Operation Bootstrap looked good on paper, its success depended on the massive entry of foreign capital into Puerto Rico. That capital would prove difficult to recruit and, once recruited, impossible to regulate. The diversified economy fell to the economic whims of big business.

"Contrary to popular thinking," Badillo writes, "Americans were reluctant to invest in Puerto Rico."[32] And those who did had problems staying there, probably because they were under-capitalized in the beginning. One-third of the small factories which opened in the early 1950s closed six or seven years later, and the hoped for diversification of smaller factories never took place. Instead, dozens of factories from certain industries (like the needle industries) were introduced through "word of mouth" among business owners. Since Americans controlled the banks and most of the capital, almost all the industry that moved to the island was linked to large banks through loans or interlocking directorships. Both the factories and the banks were U.S. companies and the banks clearly favored large, mainland-based corporations over island companies, citing stability and credit rating as reasons for this favoritism.

Since Puerto Rico had just emerged from a period of economic near-disaster, few island businesses had good credit ratings or a history of stability. Once their initial capital was spent, small businesses were forced to close. And the Commonwealth failed to use what little power it had to help. "Perhaps the best example is the Government Development Bank, set up to provide loans for industrial development," Badillo writes. "In the private sector, it functioned mainly to reinforce the local banking system. Moreover, the DB's own loan policy mirrored that of the private banks."[33] A Planning Board report for the 1940s and early 1950s shows that only 12 percent of the money lent to private investment went for manufacturing—the theoretical basis of "Bootstrap"—the rest went to real estate and commercial operations.[34]

At the same time, during the mid- and late-1950s, a unique

merchandising problem arose to exacerbate this corporate redlin-
ing. The billboards and signs in Puerto Rico tell the story, lauding
the virtues of U.S. chain stores and retail establishments. Puerto
Rico's disfigurement was not scenic alone. By the 1960s, U.S. retail
chains had almost totally taken over the retail market, virtually
eliminating local storeowners. Moreover, wholesalers—who
brought in packaged and fresh food products—were all American
since they alone could get bank loans as seed capital for their
purchases (in a business where seed capital is of tremendous
importance). These Americans did what was natural: they sought
food products from U.S. wholesalers who handle contracts in
dozens of U.S. cities as well as in Puerto Rico; they were not going
to sign separate contracts with Puerto Rican chicken farmers
when they had a national contract with Frank Perdue. Today the
stores, with few exceptions, are filled with American goods. Puerto
Ricans find it difficult to purchase fruits, vegetables, or canned
goods made and grown on their own fertile island. While Puerto
Rican commerce disappeared, investment by smaller American
companies came to a virtual standstill. Most small and middle-
sized firms had come to Puerto Rico to take advantage of the
seventeen-year tax breaks but, by the early 1970s, those tax break
agreements had run their course and the companies, already bit-
ten by galloping inflation in the United States, had no reason to
stay on the island. Small manufacturing became history. In 1966,
there were 660 factories of all sizes and twice as many retail
outlets, not counting family-run stores. Ten years later, there were
about half as many in each category. The same was true of industrial construction. Once buildings were completed, the jobs disappeared (the traditional fate of construction work) and, with little
expansion into the countryside, few new jobs were available.
    The smaller firms were not the only ones to suffer as a result of
inflation. The petroleum industry, once the island's giant, was
ravaged by world inflation and the determination by the oil producing countries to fix prices at realistic market levels. Mobil and
Exxon, two firms which maintained major refineries on the
island, began cutting back on their shifts. While both companies
continue to refine oil in Puerto Rico today, the refineries on the
island have been reduced to about one-third of their output. (The
average for U.S. mainland refineries in the bad petroleum year of
1982 was 66 percent of capacity.) And, for the most part, the plants
have become little more than stopping points for oil shipments on
their way to the United States or distribution points for products to
be consumed in Puerto Rico.[35] In fact, the Commonwealth Oil

Refining Corporation (CORCO), a consortium of U.S. refining companies run under an umbrella which represented one of the few Operation Bootstrap attempts to go into heavy industry, went bankrupt in 1982.

Still, the greatest casualties of all were the country's fishing industry and agriculture. Battered by the favoritism which the large supermarkets afforded large meat, poultry, and produce distributors, and drained of all capital investment, small Puerto Rican farmers and fishermen could not make ends meet. Fields of cane, pineapples, and other tropical fruits were left to rot, their stench rising above the fields in virtually every section of the island. There was no one to harvest, store, and sell it. With few exceptions, the fishing industry has gone the same route.

"The folly of trying to build an entire economy using foreign capital as the basis ended in almost total fiasco," claims a report from a University of Puerto Rico economist, "[but] it would be erroneous to say the American economic planners made mistakes. Their primary interest was the maximization of profit and they have attained that goal eminently."[36]

The Other Side

The island never achieved diversification. Unemployment never dropped below 10 percent, even with all the scams and schemes for population removal. For the Puerto Rican people, Operation Bootstrap was a failure. But for the large industrial concerns and their patrons, U.S. banks, it was a resounding success. While the number of investors was cut in half from 1960 to 1975, gross profit on the island jumped from $450 million to more than $1 billion a year. Most of that profit was, and still is, being made by two U.S. giants: the petrochemical and the pharmaceutical industries.

The unique character of these two production systems makes the island particularly suited to them since they are compartmentalized industries, broken down in stages which require widely different facilities and different types of work. "By the time the pharmaceutical firms started manufacturing drugs in Puerto Rico," a study team from the North American Congress on Latin America writes, "they were modern, complex organizations, as were their counterparts in other industries... Production, now only one aspect of the firms' operations, was separated from research:

sales and marketing, distribution and accounting, and other control functions also evolved into separate but coordinated operations."[37] It was more profitable for these industries to locate parts of their production processes—the most costly and polluting parts—in a country whose environmental laws were less rigid and whose labor was cheaper. Puerto Rico was ideal.

The twenty most powerful pharmaceutical corporations now have plants in Puerto Rico, brought there during the 1960s and early 1970s. These include the better known giants like Warner Lambert, Johnson and Johnson, and UpJohn as well as the lesser known, but just as powerful, hospital drug manufacturers like Merck and Syntax. They came to Puerto Rico for the tax breaks and cheap labor. They came to Puerto Rico for profit.

In five years, between 1973 and 1978, overall profits increased by over 400 percent to over $1 billion yearly, according to government documents.[38] According to the *Wall Street Journal* of September 1980, the profit-to-cost ratio for these firms was forty to one, the highest in U.S. capitalism. For every dollar a Puerto Rican drug worker makes, he or she produces forty dollars for the company.[39] These are windfall profits without taxation and the accounting wizards employed by these firms have ingenious ways of using Puerto Rico as a tax shelter for all their profits. One popular ploy is to have the mainland home office sell raw materials to the island-based subsidiaries at a very low price. In return, they buy back and subsequently sell the refined product at an extremely inflated cost. The subsidiary lists the huge profit as island profit, which is exempt from taxes. According to NACLA research, for example, UpJohn's subsidiary in Arecibo charges its parent company $600,000 for 81,500 ambules of cleocin phosphate which it packages from raw materials—bought from UpJohn's main office at $67,793.[40]

While pharmaceuticals are the most extreme example of tax breaks and profits, they are not the whole picture. Puerto Rico is today the fifth largest consumer of U.S. goods in the world, buying a total of $3.6 billion in 1977, a figure which has risen by 10 percent yearly since 1965. It also yields half the profit made by U.S. businesses in all of Latin America, the seventh largest profit made by Americans in any country in the world, and it yields this profit with fairly modest investment. "The profit intensity of the island continues to present a solid picture for those businesses investing there," said the *Wall Street Journal* in a front page brief. "There is a four-to-one profit and salary ratio throughout the island...which equalled the ratio between salary and tax breaks...for every worker who earned $10,000, the company received $40,000 in tax breaks. For every $20,000 invested, the company made $80,000."[41]

The list of investors in Puerto Rico reads like a "Who's Who" of U.S. capitalism as "quality companies" establish themselves in this perfect profit haven. General Electric produces electrical products at eight super-plants scattered throughout Puerto Rico. That company is controlled by several major banks, including Chase Manhattan and Morgan-Guaranty which also share control of Mobil with Citibank of New York. Citibank controls Phillips (owners of several petrochemicals) as well as Kennicot Copper (which has continually tried to get permission to dig up the island's mountain section for its rich copper deposits). Morgan-Guaranty also controls First Boston Corporation, which writes most of the government's public bonds, and Coca-Cola, which has no plant in Puerto Rico but does have a lot of billboards and signs.*

The list could go on: Borden's Dairy, Westinghouse, B.F. Goodrich. The point is that, contrary to the image of a tiny island where small businesses from dying sections of the mainland have taken refuge, Puerto Rico is headquarters for some of the world's most powerful financial concerns.

In an economy that produces what it does not consume and consumes what it does not produce, these companies control over 95 percent of all capital investment and all production. Even a so-called "island industry," like the Puerto Rican Power Authority, *La Autoridad de Fuertes Fluviales* (AFF), is little more than a front. In 1981, AFF reports indicate, the Authority sold 47 percent of its electricity to the island's large industrial concerns. One would assume that rates and rate increases are decided by the company before getting approval from the government. In 1979, the company's Board of Directors included the president of the island operations for Texaco, officials from several petrochemical concerns, and the vice-president of CORCO, an American.

There is, of course, nothing unique or illegal in these arrangements. Indeed, in the context of capitalism, this is an intelligent way of doing things. But it is not the economy the PPD said it was bringing to the island, nor is it the promise of Operation Bootstrap.

The Big Base

While profits flowed and economic spasms pounded Puerto Rico, there was one constant—the U.S. military and its bases. They have been the one constant since the United States took over Puerto Rico.

*These relationships, traced in the late 1970s and early 1980s, are constantly changing with the current rash of mergers and acquisitions.

As can be expected in any colony, however, the role of those bases has changed as the military policies of the United States changed. During the world wars, for example, the bases were stationing and basic training facilities for U.S. troops. During Korea and Vietnam, when recruitment from Puerto Rico itself became intense, they were home to soldiers from the island and at the same time provided access to the beachfront areas on which to practice new invasionary techniques.

Puerto Rico, in short, has always been militarily useful. Over the last ten years, however, it has become militarily crucial and that is because there has been a shift in U.S. military attention from Southeast Asia to Latin America and the Caribbean.

Under President Ronald Reagan, Washington has developed one of the most aggressively militaristic policies in the hemisphere's history. There is, of course, a long history of covert action against revolutionary movements and progressive governments in Latin America and the Caribbean, and there is some history of direct invasion, as is the case with the Dominican Republic in 1965. But never has the U.S. government so brazenly carried on so many battles in so many countries simultaneously. There are many explanations for this intensified belligerence, but for Puerto Rico, the policy has resulted in an unprecedented militarization of the island.

Today in Puerto Rico and Vieques (the small satellite island-municipality), there are over twenty active military installations; they literally form a string around the entire island and cover about 75 percent of Vieques' land. The bases are part of a Pentagon program to expand the military use of Puerto Rico.

While the expansion of the facilities is important in and of itself, what is more important is the transformation of Puerto Rico into the principal U.S. military base in Latin America. Not only is it a training facility for "marine to land counter-insurgency," but apparently it is now the principal staging point for such missions. Carlos Zenon, then president of the Vieques Fishermen's Association, calls his island "a military bridge between the United States and the rest of the hemisphere." The bridge was used during the Grenada invasion, for example, which was rehearsed in Vieques two years before it occurred. When the invasion order was finally given in 1983, U.S. troops actually embarked from staging points on Vieques' beaches. The same is true for almost all the many incursions by U.S. warships into Nicaraguan waters.

The situation provokes another concern among environmentalists and activists. Because of the increase in the military use of Puerto Rico, the United States has increased its storage of high-tech weaponry in the western section of the island. No one is sure just what this weaponry is—some activists insist that some of it is nuclear; the island government denies that, and the Pentagon never comments. But nuclear or not, the bombs stored in the facilities which blanket large sections of the less-populated western side of the island represent a real threat to the physical security of the island.

Given current U.S. policy, it is clear that for the near future, Puerto Rico's importance as a strategic base in Latin America will increase.

What is most obvious about what has happened to Puerto Rico is that it so profoundly contradicts the PPD's promises. In the early years, Munoz stated: "As statehood is impossible, the only alternative from colonialism is independence. Autonomy can only be fraudulent...a decorous and decorative blanket which covers the rag of colonialism and that assumes the goal of independence."[42] Who knows if, in his later years, Munoz remembered that quote or whether he erased from his mind the nagging realization of his essential failure. Still, Populism's failure was not one of miscalculation or misunderstanding: the Populists clearly turned their backs on the thinking contained in that quote. For the right to govern their country, they betrayed its best interests.

If early on they did not see why their brand of development was not in the country's best interest, they surely must have seen it later. Because today Puerto Rico is being destroyed in virtually every sense.

4

The Dream Deferred

The Sign on the Factory

There's a point where the main road of the beach town of Luqillo intersects with the highway to Mayaguez. The road travels through a tunnel of fifty-foot tall rubber trees, past a stream whose water has been condemned. At that point, the roads meet and there's a string of produce stalls, each offering mangoes from Vieques and Salinas, *viandas* and *platanos* brought from abroad, and other fruits piled up on wooden display stands flanked by curtains of cellophane-wrapped coconut candy.

Shoppers come in droves, lugging children, pulling carts, or carrying bags, to bicker over the prices and squeeze, smell, and examine the fruit. They stock up for the week on the kinds of products that are now scarce on an island which once produced more than the people could eat.

Next to those stands there is a metal fence with a yellow sign hanging on it. The drawing on the sign shows a man with a hardhat flexing his biceps—the symbol of Operation Bootstrap. The lettering reads: "Another project of FOMENTO." Behind that sign is a burnt shell of a building which was once the small factory the sign brags about.

Where workers once entered there's a hole larger than a trailer truck; the wall, partly burned away, is mostly decayed and rotted.

67

Where they once stood to do their work and earn their money, there is only half a floor, stinking of rotten wood, rat excrement, and dead vermin. Where there once stood the symbol of industrialization, progress, and hope, there now stands a useless, decaying eyesore.

"See that," one of the storeowners, Jose Molina said, "That's a haunted house...only the ghosts moved away."

Jose Molina was fifty years old when he said that. Each day he would arrive at five in the morning at his vegetable stall to pull out his display boxes and pack the fruit and the vegetables, carefully hanging the stacks of *platanos*, long strings of candy, and the *guiros* carved out of tree bark which formed the stall's facade.

Molina's hands were strong and stained brown. "I don't think they would stain the produce anymore," he said. "The stain is inside my skin. It was inside my father's and my father's father's." For those three generations, and many more, the Molinas were leather workers and shoemakers by trade. Jose Molina's father, worked for decades in a small shoe shop outside their wooden home in Luqillo. "I could have taken the shop and gotten by," Molina said, hauling a stalk of bananas that must have weighed fifty pounds on one of his shoulders. "But they bought that factory and I decided to take one of those jobs. They paid a lot better than a shop."

The shoe factory where Molina went to work was brought to the area through Operation Bootstrap in 1952. When it opened, the area around it came to life. All the men, and many women, could now find jobs which paid several times what they made before. "The people were so happy," Molina remembered. "They all started going to church to thank God that Munoz Marin was born. It was that way for nearly ten years in this area."

Then something happened which Jose Molina, himself a businessman, cannot explain. He can only describe it. "One morning—it was Tuesday morning and I remember it was very slow— we had finished a large order and I was just fixing this frame where I had a picture of my wife and daughter. Just nailing these small nails, you understand. Well, this man, very well dressed man, who looked like he had just stopped running, very agitated, walked into the shop. The foreman screamed at us to stop working, which was okay with me because—even though I don't like to stop what I'm doing—it was just a frame for myself. This man introduced himself as Watson and told us that he was a 'field representative' for the company we were working for. We all applauded because he looked important and was a field representative from the United States and, anyway, he used the foreman to translate so he spoke only English, which we thought was the sky itself.

"But Watson told us that, in one month, his company was engineering an 'operations transfer.' Our factory would be moved. If we were willing, we could get a job in the new site. Someone asked him where it was. 'North Carolina,' he says. Some of the workers thought he was talking about Carolina the town. They said it would be too far to travel every morning. But I had been in the service and I knew where he was talking about."

Jose Molina sat down and wiped his brow:

> Things weren't the same after that. The area started losing people; they went away looking for jobs...this was about 1963 or '64. And many Americans began moving in to buy second homes near the beach. All of my friends are gone from here. I have only that smelly ruin of a factory.
>
> If you want to know how it burned, I can only tell you that one night a group of workers got drunk. They broke into the factory while it was still operating, beat up a guard and piled thousands of shoes to the ceiling, a mountain of leather. They threw kerosene all over it and lit it. The stench was so strong that the dogs in the neighborhood went crazy, running up and down the road, so sickened by the stench that they vomited but so frightened by the fire they couldn't stand still.
>
> And that's what I remember. We all thought our prayers had been answered...we were wrong. It's like a dream which starts up beautifully and one knows he's going to rest well and then it turns into a nightmare and in the morning one doesn't even want to begin the day.

The spectacular failure of the promise of Operation Bootstrap—its inability to build a balanced and progressive economy—left many closed factories. "As the tax break grants began to expire, wages were on the rise, not so much relative to the United States, but in comparison to new centers of low-wage production in the third world," NACLA scholars write. "Mutual tariff reductions negotiated between the United States and its major trading partners began to dim the appeal of investing within the U.S. tariff barriers. All this put into question further employment-generating manufacturing investment..."[1] And it hurt no one more than the Puerto Rican people, often left by the process with little more than unpunched time cards.

As with Molina's factory, textile and electrical goods manufacturers and other intermediate producers began "moving their operations" in the early 1970s to the southern United States or consolidating the operations of several factories into one or two mainland plants. Because of inflation and other economic problems in the United States, the need for Puerto Rican labor had become minimal. Once again, the Puerto Rican worker was discarded. By the beginning of the 1970s, the emotion most prominent on the island was hysteria linked to unemployment. Today, the hysteria has turned into near resignation.

Since World War II, the people of Licha's island have never had it so bad. Government figures show over 25 percent of the labor force unemployed; the real figure is probably much larger since official statistics don't include those who haven't ever looked for work or have stopped looking. As a better measure of unemployment, a 1977 University of Puerto Rico economic study group found that, of 950,000 working-age people, 400,000 didn't have jobs—over 40 percent.[2] It's logical to believe that figure has grown in the intervening years.

The unemployment problem is combined, in this scenario of collapse, with several other problems. Wages, for instance, have remained extremely low. The average Puerto Rican family of four earns less than $10,000 a year, lower than families in any other area within U.S. control. The per capita wage is about $3.40 an hour, about 60 percent what it is on the mainland.[3]

To make matter's worse, Puerto Rico suffers the lashes of a spectacular inflation, 18 percent higher than in the United States. Because consumer goods are made on the mainland (or at the very least, channeled through it), retail prices in Puerto Rico always include substantial transportation costs. As with any captive market, there is no need to control this pass-along since there's no competition from other exporting countries. So Puerto Ricans pay for the goods, pay for the additional shipping, and probably pay a bit more just for extra corporate pocket-padding.

Inflation's impact is deepened by another colonial inheritance; Puerto Rico is today a society immersed in the culture of consumerism, among the most conspicuous in Latin America. In part, the consumerism is a by-product of the island's development. People in a modern industrial society are going to want its artifacts. They will not be satisfied to live life without kitchen appliances, televisions, and radios when such appliances are so readily available. Buying a washing machine or television becomes, for the poor, a way of hiding their poverty from themselves, if not from others.

But in reality, poor people *do* need televisions and radios. Given the price of live entertainment, it's doubtful that most working-class people are going to frequent movies every week or go see live shows. The live bands which perform in the Condado area nightclubs are not catering to an audience which was working in a factory two hours before. For the worker then, the only viable entertainment option is television.

Cars are no more luxuries than televisions and radios. This is no longer a horse-and-buggy society. Industry always brings with it a strict demand for promptness which agriculture inherently found unnecessary. It makes little difference to a harvest whether you start working half an hour later but, in a factory, such tardiness would spell assembly line chaos.

So promptness, made possible by high-speed driving, is essential and, among the achievements brought to the island by the Commonwealth is a road system which is among the finest in Latin America. Since the public transportation system is almost non-existent, people have to drive cars.

The high cost of these goods means that the consumer society has become a society of credit. Stores offer credit with stunningly liberal terms to anyone who will buy more than $100 of furniture or appliances. "Paying off" is the most prominent aspect of the Puerto Rican working-class family's budget. "In fact, the mere offer of credit isn't enough," former Resident Commissioner Jaime Benitez said, "Stores must actively advertise their credit policy more than they advertise what they are actually selling."[4]

This spiral of credit dependence is complimented, in the rainbow of Puerto Rican problems, by the dependence on food stamps. Employed or not, over 80 percent of the Puerto Rican people qualify for the federal food stamp program and 70 percent actually receive food stamps every month to help them cope with the island's enormous economic problems. Since the program started, *voy a los cupones* ("I'm going to the stamps") has become a part of the popular vernacular. The program itself costs about $3 billion a year.

"The Food Stamp Scandal" is what WCBS-TV's popular *Sixty Minutes* show called the situation.[5] In tones ranging from barely concealed resentment to astonishment, the reporter laid out the scandal: Americans, she explained, were paying a kind of welfare state wage to the Puerto Rican people. It was the only incidence, she explained, where federally tax-based food programs were benefiting a non-American country.

The perception that food stamps are a way for Puerto Ricans to get something for nothing isn't new, nor is it confined to journalists. W.R. Grace, the shipping magnate asked by President Reagan in 1982 to evaluate government efficiency, called food stamps "a Puerto Rican program." That, of course, is not true. Most food stamp recipients are welfare recipients and most welfare recipients are white Americans. Even in proportion to U.S. residents, Puerto Ricans living in the United States make up no higher percentage of food stamp recipients than any other minority population and what's more, the incidence of public assistance can be attributed, not to some greedy plot, but to economic deprivation. The logic that this is some kind of "foreign" use of these funds is equally fallacious, since Puerto Ricans are citizens of the United States. But there lies the difficulty in the argument. For those who denounce the food stamp program are absolutely right, they just arrive at that point for all the wrong reasons.

American taxpayers are being hustled but not by the people of Puerto Rico. The food stamp program on the island is a way of diffusing an explosion, avoiding the Harlem, Detroit, or Watts uprisings in a country which would seem prone to them. Puerto Rico, after all, is always depressed and always hot. Piven and Cloward describe such programs as "designed to mute civil disorder."[6] The psychological impact is powerful.

"When I first saw what we had bought with the stamps," a young teacher who returned to the island after living in the states for six years said, "I cried because I never thought you could buy so much food with so little. But I cried for another reason: my people were living like this off someone else. We become an island of beggars and beggars seldom seek their own freedom."

An Island is Dying

"I am the first person in my family to get past grade school. If you don't understand what that means, you'll never understand how I think."

Fernando Cabrera spends eight hours a day turning little screws. He bends over, his slightly lined, brown face a study in relaxed concentration as his long fingers grip the screwdriver and slowly turn it. His eyes glance frequently at the dials above the screws. When the needle on the dial hits its desired mark, Cabrera smiles.

"I never make a mistake on those. That's why this plant is still here. Too much on one screw and the whole place could go up." Fernando Cabrera is forty-four years old. He is a mechanical engineer, in charge of maintaining the machinery in one section of one of the area's giant petrochemical plants.

"When you think of this industry, some people have the image that everybody's working hard, sweating and making petro-chemicals," he said with a boyish laugh, gentle and charming, "But the machinery produces the chemicals...the workers keep the machinery going. We're all technicians...most industrial workers are technicians. It's not a muscle job alone...you have to know. I am one of this country's journeyman mechanics on this type of machinery; one of five or six."

Cabrera says he's confident in his job because he knows it. And he has a little help. "I wear this everyday." He pointed to his gold medal with the Sacred Heart on it. "This is my protection. I know if something were to happen to me, it is God's will. Do you think he would unwillingly allow his own medal to be blown up?" He stopped to think. "Of course, the medal might survive some kind of fire here, but in most cases not even gold could survive an explosion intact. If you looked around you and saw what the fumes from this plant do! Even with the nose clip you have on, your nostrils will continue to sting. You know that any explosion would totally destroy this area. God knows that since he knows every-thing, so I'll never die. But, to be sure, I concentrate when I turn those screws."

Over the last decade, the southern city of Ponce where Cabrera and his family live, has changed. Before the turn of the century, Ponce was the home of the sugar plantation owners; they built stately wooden homes with balconies of ornate metal work, tile floors, and windows with wood-carved mosaics in their sills. It still retains some of that flavor: the dignified air of a city of masters.

But Ponce is also the major urban center in the south of the island. And all that has come to the cities has come to Ponce. Cars form traffic jams along Avenida Misericordia, the city's main street, at all times of the day; their angry horns and carbon monox-ide fill the streets. People rush around as frenzied as in any U.S. city, not even stopping to greet each other as they walk by. And there are the groups of young people who are out of work, out of school, out of hopes and future. Some are incapable of saying anything; they're stoned, their minds dancing to the tune that floats into their veins from the end of a needle. Others peddle drugs openly, or make fun of passers-by. They are a nuisance and a symbol of what has happened to Ponce, and to Puerto Rico.

At the time, Fernando Cabrera's oldest son was in jail and his second oldest was one of those kids on the street corners. "He's in a

program to cure the habit," Cabrera says. "But it doesn't seem to
do him much good."

Cabrera sat down, taking off his hardhat and pulling out a
cigarette. "We did everything, his mother and I. We gave him
everything he needed. We lit candles in the church, told him to talk
to the priest. We brought his grandfather to the city to talk to him
and give him wisdom. We had the older people from the neighborhood talk to him...even the leader of the PNP in this area talked to
him. No good."

Cabrera took a drag from his cigarette and the thoughts
rushed across his face. "When I was a kid, I used to love to climb
trees. I would go up to a different tree each day with a knife and cut
niches in my footsteps so that I could never repeat a tree. My youth
was spent climbing every tree I could find, branch by branch,
sometimes for hours, until I was high enough to satisfy myself, so
high that the only niches on that tree were mine.

"I told myself when I married that my son would climb higher
than my niches. Now so many of those trees are gone and so is my
son."

Fernando Cabrera's world is a microcosm of the promises and
failures of Operation Bootstrap. As a skilled worker with a good
salary, working in an industry whose size and power reach far
beyond the dreams of even the most optimistic economic planners
of the 1950s, he represents the fulfillment of the "Bootstrap"
dream. But because his industry has contributed to the degeneration of the island's physical environment and because his personal life has been virtually destroyed by the social environment,
he also dramatizes the indictment that can be leveled against
Operation Bootstrap.

As its boosters are quick to point out, it has modernized Puerto
Rico and made the island an industrial center whose importance
to the United States and, by extension to the world, is inestimable.
In fact, in a limited sense, it is just what Munoz Marin claimed he
was seeking: the program which organized an infra-structure
through which Puerto Rico could one day be truly independent.
But, as its many detractors counter, it has also destroyed so much
of the physical potential of the island that independence becomes
less attainable day by day. Puerto Rico, scientists say, stands
before the world as one of its most industrially ravaged countries.

Federal environmental laws apply to Puerto Rico but, like so
many laws, their effectiveness depends largely on the willingness
of local officials to enforce them. In Puerto Rico, where the
government's orientation is to soothing industry's problems rather

than creating them, such enforcement is rare. And the impact is staggering.

"An island of this size is like a fish tank," biologist and environmentalist Neftali Garcia said, during an interview. "All the components must be balanced. If one gets too large, everything is upset."[7]

This is the case with heavy industry. It has been concentrated in certain parts of the island, often too close to water and in many cases has overtaken the water and raised its temperature. It has dirtied the air and has, as a result, ruined portions of the agriculture. It is killing people and destroying parts of Puerto Rico. In the southern area, from Catano to Guayanilla, there are more refineries, petrochemical, and pharmaceutical plants per resident than anywhere else in the world, according to the Federal Environmental Protection Agency.[8]

One summer afternoon a group of journalists took a tour of this area of the country from which the trees with Fernando's niches have disappeared. As we drove along the highway outside of Ponce the long stretches of petroleum refineries were busy coughing up their last smoke of the day. The heat was tremendous, some five degrees hotter in the immediate vicinity of the CORCO plant, and the surrounding area—barren as the moonscape—added to the feeling of stifling heat.

The heat from the petrochemicals boiled the water and made steam inside the mountain. Our guide, a UPR economist said, "It ate away at the roots and in four years killed the plants and baked the dirt. That is not sand you see, it's dirt clay baked white. If you were to try to walk up that mountain, the soles would burn off your shoes."

Then what about the pineapple fields on the other side which were once famous for their yield? "Ah, take a look." What we saw on the other side of those mountains was unrecognizable. Stalks rose like wooden picks in the dirt, not resembling trees in any way and the ground was covered with something that looked like human skin giving off the stench of garbage.

"These crops are so powerful that they continue to bear fruit, but the fruit comes off rotten. Something like being in a greenhouse and turning on the heat so that the roots begin to cook. The cooked roots, underground, are powerful but not powerful enough. This field would yield about half a million pineapples a season."

But he told us that the stench was not from the fruit. "That's the stench from the industry plants you smell. A government biologist came here once and made a report that was never

released. He said that living here reduced life expectancy by
twenty years. The contamination is so strong that it wipes out
your lungs and burns the hair inside your nose. My doctors tell me
to move, but where would I go without a job?"

Although no comprehensive study has ever been done by the
government, a doctor's study shows a higher rate of lung and
throat cancer in this area than island-wide. In Guayanilla, for
example, 19 percent of the population suffer from obstructed
respiratory illness, and in Catano, 50 percent suffer similar throat
illness.[9]

Sometimes factory pollution, particularly from the petrochemical plants, takes on gruesome proportions. In 1975, for
example, gas from a chemical plant in the middle of the island
escaped. Over the next year workers began reporting surprising
results. The breasts of men began developing and women workers
started growing facial hair. Even the length of vocal cords were
altered.[10]

The irony was that the island government's Workman's Compensation Board refused any compensation or even an investigation. "We only investigate accidents which keep a person from
working," a spokesman commented. "A man with breasts can
work to say nothing of a woman with a moustache. I even know a
few myself."[11] But the joke was lost on those affected, as it was lost
on those seventy petro-chemical workers who are terminally ill
because of mercury poisoning discovered in their blood. They have
already begun to die from leukemia or heart attacks. "Their
blood," an official said, "is just no good." "They are unfortunate,"
another husky Pittsburgh Plate Glass mechanic said in 1975, "but
it was an accident. I don't need an accident." He showed his
hands, the fingers swollen to twice their normal size and the palms
the color of a brilliant sunset. "The blood is forced by the pressure
of the air to come up. If I don't wear gloves, it hurts everytime I
touch something."

"It's tough to understand what that means when you don't
live here," Fernando Cabrera once said. "But look at your hands."
They were trembling and sweaty. "Now look to your right." On the
right side were rows of four story buildings, fronted by single
family homes, all concrete, all the same like so much of the architecture of Puerto Rico. They looked like desert outposts, surrounded by hot wind-swept sand and perpetually cloudy skies.
"Your hands are shaking because the atmosphere has changed
your body temperature radically. The people who live in those
houses no longer have shaking hands...their systems have ad-

justed. They are scheduled, on the average, to die ten years before you do."

"Besides the leaks, which are almost monthly in those plants," says Federal Environmental Protection Agency scientist Rick Cahill, "the main danger is that there are so many of them lined up. Industry argues that pollution is a necessary evil but that it's not harmful because there's not enough of it. Well, that might be true for one or two plant sites. But there are over ten in the southern area alone. That is industrial murder."[12]

If the fish could talk, they would probably agree. "Some men deserve to die," Dona Licha said, "but what court has condemned the fish?" The debacle of the waves of death in 1974, with thousands of fish washed up on the shore, covered with oil and so hot the human hand couldn't touch them, was apparently produced by leaks of chemicals and petro-chemicals which soiled and heated the water. They were the product of an accident.

Accidents do happen whenever industry operates. But a nation should expect of its industry some care and consideration in its waste disposal procedures; Puerto Rico can expect all it wants but care and consideration just don't come.

The reliance on nature to dispose of poisons has dire consequences. In Manati, for example, the pharmaceuticals dump their waste into the beautiful Manati River, which carries the liquid waste into the ocean. Fishermen reported a smelly, thick, brown liquid from both the Merck and Bristol Myers plants. The river spawned lush vegetation, making it almost impossible to navigate, and extremely odorous. According to the *New York Times* in April 1976, a haul of 4,000 pounds of fish—normal during the 1960s—was now reduced to 40 pounds and expensive nets, designed to last a decade, had to be replaced each year.[13]

But there are continuous effects. "The water is often ten degrees hotter because of the presence of those plants," said biologist Garcia. "And the water contains chemicals whose proportions are such that, were this any place in the United States, they would immediately ban fish from the market. You have sulfur, mercury in incredible proportions and even some chemical neutralizers that in reasonable quantities cause cancer."[14]

One environmentalist study group did a review of the marine life in the area in 1976. They found that season by season, between 1955 and 1975, the fish population had been reduced by 10 percent. "There will always be fish," Dona Licha said. "They come from God. But since God's no dope, he's going to tell them to go elsewhere and not come here to be poisoned." She laughs bitterly.

"Maybe he'll just send a few so the owners of the factory could get cancer."

Biologist Garcia's concern is also technical. "Besides the destruction of the physical beauty and of life, this is a disaster area economically. The destroyed fish make the building of a fishing industry almost impossible; any island without a fishing industry is untenable economically."

Studies of agriculture and fishing in Puerto Rico, show that it could feed its population five times over—a fact cited in 1980 by conservative columnist William F. Buckley, hardly an independence advocate—but, with the destruction of crops, that won't be the case in ten years. Unworked land loses its fertility.[15] So industrialization has become a self-fulfilling prophecy.

To place the problem in perspective, one-fifth of all Puerto Ricans live near the southern idustrial belt or one of the pollution-producing enclaves all over the island. The Environmental Protection Agency says they confront "a health damaging situation each day."[16] Although much of Puerto Rico is threatened by some pollution, the amount of heavy industry in the south makes it the showcase for destruction. Indeed, it is safe to say that the middle mountain region will never suffer this fate and much of the north will remain relatively isolated from it. But the southern region was once the sugar capital of the world, producing more than 60 percent of the island's local produce, and was Puerto Rico's most important fishing area. The land was the best, the water most productive, but all of this is being destroyed. "When this is gone," Garcia says, "the potential for feeding ouselves will have disappeared."[17]

Tourism

These large industries are not the only economic components which have affected Puerto Rico. The tourist industry, the island's major generator of capital, must take its place in the arsenal of destruction. While other industries might ravage the land, air, and water with pollution, tourism concentrates on the beaches and the minds of the Puerto Rican people. It is in a sense just as destructive.

Tourism is responsible for nearly 30 percent of the gross national product of Puerto Rico according to 1983 government estimates.[18] It is a major priority of the commonwealth offices in other countries, all of which have tourism departments, and is the pride and joy of the government.

Tourism's physical artifacts are a string of hotels, mainly in the Condado section of the island and near the Isla Verde area where the airport stands. "We would be a country of fools, if we didn't encourage tourism," one Commonwealth Department of Tourism spokesman said. Tourism represents one of the major sources of revenues in most developed countries and is quickly becoming so in much of the underdeveloped world. For countries where underdevelopment bears at least one fruit—unspoiled environments—tourism is a constructive industry. But, in Puerto Rico, there are different aspects to tourism. There are the Condado hotels, which line the water in the island's major hotel area—relatively close to San Juan—where property values are highest in Puerto Rico. The hotels are all American owned, of course, and most of the money leaves Puerto Rico. The hotel chains have bought beachfront property, large sections of land where only their residents can sit back and bask in the sun. As a result of a campaign led by *independentistas*, there's a law that any Puerto Rican can use those beaches if they can get to them, but the beaches are accessible only through the hotels and the hotels are protected by guards.

Those hotels offer a whole gamut of night life to their patrons, from restaurants and shows to the ultimate in pleasurable pain: casino gambling. To walk through one of these casinos is to forget one is in Puerto Rico. In fact, that is the case with the whole Condado. It is not really Puerto Rican at all. Its commercial streets are lined with small souvenir shops, typical of urban tourist traps or national parks souvenir stands, and with restaurants that supposedly offer "Puerto Rican cuisine," which is the island's food bastardized into what owners feel is suited to American tastes. English is spoken almost exclusively and, for the most part, it is difficult to find a Puerto Rican face but for sales personnel, hotel workers, and waiters—all of whom have mastered English, the language of their tips.

"Tourism has brought to Puerto Rico the social squalor reminiscent of pre-revolutionary Havana," Maldonado Denis writes. "Prostitution, gaming, and every form of diversion not acceptable in the societies of the mother country is practiced openly when not legally in the tourist sections of the island."[19]

The "meat trade," both male and female, is part of the services offered by many of the area bars, almost all of which have had to bring in nude dancing shows to compete with the high quality night clubs which have offered at least partial nudity in their shows for decades. Smartly dressed young Puerto Rican men and women can be seen at all hours of the day in hotels and casinos, walking up to rich-looking American tourists, introducing themselves and following up with a quick proposition.

It is common to see American tourists with young natives on their arms attending the Condado's nightclubs and bars, and escort services, whose phone numbers are now readily available in the local directory, have tripled over the last ten years, according to the island-wide vice squad. Yet, records show, there is seldom an arrest for prostitution and those which do occur are related to some act of violence perpetrated by the prostitute.

The real harm brought to Puerto Rico by this tourism is more considerable than the social squalor. This is dependent tourism, the kind of tourism which poses a significant argument for the continuation of colonialism. Rather than emphasize the strengths of the country, like European and other Latin American countries do, Puerto Rico emphasizes its own weakness, its chameleon-like character, its ability to mimic the tourist stereotype and realize the tourists' dreams.

On this foundation is built one of the island's most economically important industries. An independent Puerto Rico would, of course, never engage in such tourism. It's not the tourism of an independent people and so, if such tourism is to continue, colonialism must continue. And, since there are many thousands of people who earn their livelihoods through such tourism (many of whom are managers and planners), that population is certain to favor colonialism's perpetuation.

"Mean Streets"

Fernando Cabrera's son is probably like the kids who hang out near the Rio Piedras "marketplace," an enormous center of food stores, novelty shops, and open air kiosks which sell the products of local craftspeople. The marketplace is busy during the day and early evening, as people with cash come to buy. That's what draws the kids. They wait for likely victims, steal their money, and disappear into the crowds of the marketplace. The rest of the time, they coast between the extremes of euphoric calm and violent "pre-fix" anxiety, occasionally staring at some passer-by and hurling some obscene insult. The marketplace kids are a symbol of one of colonialism's most striking creations: criminal behavior.

Each day, *El Vocera*, Puerto Rico's sensationalist newspaper carries a front-page story about some bank robbery, shooting, or domestic homicide with an accompanying picture. Inside, in what newspapers call the "news hole," there is yet more crime news. Those accustomed to big city life in the United States would hardly bat an eyelash, but Puerto Rico used to be an island proud of its tradition of open doors and safe streets. It was, for Puerto Rican young in the United States, the place you were sent to "cool out," to get away from the criminal lure of U.S. urban areas.

That is far from the reality of Puerto Rico today. Indeed, the very existence of the paper—directed more to crimes than to the restrained mix of political news and world events typical of the island's two other papers—indicates just how bad things are. *El Vocero* was founded in the mid-1970s at the beginning of what island police feel is the period of major crime increase which victimizes Puerto Rico today.

During the past decade, crime has become one of the people's major concerns. The number of murders has increased about 5 percent a year since 1973 and robbery has grown even faster.[20] By any definition, even that of streetwise Puerto Ricans born and raised in the United States now living on the island, it's dangerous to live in Puerto Rico's larger cities. Even left-wing intellectuals and leaders, traditionally resistant to taking up the "law and order" cries of right-wingers on the island, have now come to admit that crime is an issue of major importance.

Crime creates an atmosphere—a blanket of fear and powerlessness, mistrust which verges on paranoia—which progressively destroys the social fabric by increasingly locking people into their homes and their normal routines. Because Puerto Rico is a car culture, its streets are usually empty after dark; crime has exacerbated the feelings of isolation and loneliness on those streets. The feeling of frightened alienation is symbolized by the average urban house in Puerto Rico which is now equipped with a metal grate on each door and window.

"This thing of having doors closed all the time is just not the way things were," Leonida Perez, a resident of Rio Piedras (in the San Juan area) for over fifty years said. "It used to be that your neighbor would always have the door open, would always be available, and your children would be cared for whether or not you were home. It was safe in my country; it no longer is."[21]

The emptiness of the streets has also spawned grotesque phenomena like the gangs of mad dogs which roam the streets of working-class residential areas at night. In Hato Rey, for example, police spent much of 1981 combatting gangs of thirty or more dogs which walked the streets looking for food in garbage piles and on curbsides. So accustomed were those strays to deserted nighttime streets that, when they spotted humans walking at night, they would viciously attack what they perceived as an alien rival.

It's logical that crime would grow in Puerto Rico for modern colonialism has brought with it the exaggerated inequalities of industrial society—the gaps between those who have and those who do not, linked with the lifestyle expectations which define poverty. To say that a Puerto Rican person is poor today is to say he or she enjoys no higher standard of living than that considered privileged even forty years ago—both in terms of real wages and of technology formerly earmarked for only the very wealthy. Still, there are those who have more: the people with two new cars, the people with superb clothes for every day of the month, the people who live in beachfront housing, those who can fly to New York four times a year rather than once every two years. This considerable population of haves is ever present in the eyes of the much larger population of have-nots, and the contrast in their lifestyles puts the island's widespread poverty in stark relief.

But poverty of this type has always existed. What industrialism has brought to Puerto Rico is marginalization: the mountain of human despair personified by the groups of people who are not only poor—as were the land workers of a century ago—but are poor with absolutely nothing to do.

Ironically, many of the real reforms sponsored by the commonwealth government—unemployment benefits, public assistance programs—have served to increase this marginalized population. The fact that, for the first time in Puerto Rican history, people really don't have to work to survive has destroyed the parallel economy, still prominent in Santo Domingo, of children moving in with relatives of friends to "help out" with housework and relieve the financial burden they were creating in their own homes. Any Puerto Rican neighborhood of thirty years ago would boast a number of small businesspeople who worked at everything from cleaning bottles to tending gardens for anyone willing to pay a few pennies. Those people are now on street corners.

No one argues that this underground economy was anything but an outgrowth of deprivation. But it did have two benefits: it kept people off the streets, which kept crime to a minimum, and it tended to channel their attempts at making a living into a kind of community-strengthening energy. Everyone in the neighborhood got to know everyone else under this system; it helped to mold the cultural life of the family and the community which figured so prominently for much of the agricultural proletariat's existence.

More importantly, the underground economy avoided the stinging problem of masses of people who become unaccustomed to working, who spread a disease of alienation, whose children will grow up in impoverished households where the idea of adults going to work is a foreign concept. They are part of the syndrome of generational unemployment which has afflicted U.S. black communities since the end of World War II.

It would be a mistake, however, to view the problem as confined to these marginalized people. Unemployment affects those who still hold jobs or really want them. A worker who suddenly finds a pink slip in the locker confronts the trauma of unemployment based, as Fernandez Mendez pointed out, in the working-class cultural trait of "priding work as a central source of personal value."[22] Like automobile workers in the United States, suddenly confronting lives without any prospect of work, the unemployed Puerto Rican worker faces demoralization and doubt about his or her own worth.

But in Puerto Rico, people have been facing the possibility of plant closings for over twenty years and the resulting atmosphere of trauma is the basis for what writer Ramon Arbona labels "a sense of insanity, of mediocrity and self-destruction...a sense among people that not only are they not doing well but that they cannot."[23]

The combination of factors has brought to Puerto Rico a tension which often erupts into internalized violence of the type Fanon described. Like a frustrated child banging its head on the floor, Puerto Rican society racks itself with inward anger, expressed each day.

The anger is fiercest in the city where a more "laid back" lifestyle has been replaced by tension-packed pushing and shoving, traffic jams, frequent arguments, and a more than occasional brawl. There is an obvious edge to city life that wasn't there before. A case can be made, of course, that cities are like that, and it's true that the island's countryside is calmer, more traditional, and friendlier than the cities. But what's important here is that, today, the cities play a much more important role in the economic and social life of Puerto Rico. Indeed, they are the population centers, the places people migrate to during industrialization.

Nowhere is the society's tension and violence more apparent than in the violence against women, both domestic and outside the home. In the Puerto Rican home, where women have often been the object of men's frustrations, sexual violence has doubled since 1970, according to police figures. The percentage must be higher since it's doubtful that all domestic beatings are reported.

If this doesn't indicate a rise in social tensions, the public acts of sexual aggression certainly do. Three years ago, for example, police began noticing a near epidemic of public masturbation and cases of men exposing themselves to female passers-by. Rape has also risen substantially over the last ten years and, says the logic on city streets, women simply cannot afford to walk alone at any time of the day or evening.

Women are the repository for the internalized violence of a sexist society, but females don't take the brunt of this anger alone. Incidents of family homicide (brother against brother, for example) have risen by 170 percent since 1973, according to police. "I would say most of our work is homicides between people who are close friends or family," Esteban Rivera, a homicide detective with the Hato Rey police district said. "Most take place in homes and bars and in most cases it is unexpected violence, not some kind of long standing problem or feud. For us, way over half, maybe 75 percent, is a killer who has not been involved in a physical attack before. We aren't talking about professional killers here, although we have plenty of those. We are talking about the guy who goes crazy for a moment and kills his cousin.

"There is no question for me that this kind of homicide is pretty new here. I mean we always had these kinds of problems among family members but never on the level of today. People are really crazy sometimes."[24]

And some people are really crazy all the time. In fact, in 1978, Puerto Rico ranked as the country with the highest per capita incidence of diagnosed mental illness in the world.[25] Matters are somewhat complex here because, as Chris Hansen of the American Civil Liberties Union Mental Health Project pointed out, "The definition of insanity is political and class-wise a very loaded term. You can be rich and be suffering from exhaustion but, if you're poor, they say you cracked up. You can be nuts, absolutely out of your mind, and be functioning on the streets or you can just be having a few heavy problems and be committed. It's a very, very touchy problem."[26]

Because Puerto Rico's poor population is proportionately larger than that of other industrialized countries like the United States, there is probably substantially more diagnosed insanity. The insular Health Department makes its estimates based on functional behavior: those who have stopped effectively functioning at job or home are listed as insane. Using this admittedly crude rule, the Health Department found that in 1978 about one out of every twenty-three adults in Puerto Rico was functionally irresponsible.[27] This figure is staggering when one considers that in the United States the number is closer to one in 100.

Another important reflection of social problems is the level of drug and alcohol addiction, and here Puerto Rico distinguishes itself again. It has the third highest alcoholism rate among countries in the world which measure such things. The measurement is based on a 1974 to 1978 study done by the Health Department which defines an alcoholic as a person "who drinks at least three ounces of alcohol every day and has trouble controlling the use of alcohol." It is a definition which would put most American consumers of alcohol within the classification: alcoholic. Even a definition which includes such a wide range of drinkers is useful because it profiles the amount of daily "social" level drinking which goes on in a society.[28]

The Health Department found that one out of every three adults suffers an "alcohol addiction." It accompanied its study with a survey, done by a team of physicians representing several hospitals and clinics on the island, indicating that two out of every five adults in Puerto Rico feel "irritable and depressed" if they don't drink every day.

Like so many other social problems in Puerto Rico, alcoholism is covered-up by turning it into a big joke: from TV situation comedies based on drunken men to the popular joke that "every house is worth a drink," referring to the tendency of people to immediately offer their visitors *un trago* (a drink). But the reality is very serious. For while a drunken society is obviously a society of people trying to wipe out reality, drinking in Puerto Rico has become such an integral part of the daily working-class culture that—as is the case in contemporary Cuba—it will still linger as a problem long after colonialism has disappeared.

Some fear that that is what will soon happen with drugs, yet another post-Operation Bootstrap problem. In 1977, Governor Rafael Hernandez Colon called drugs "the greatest problem facing the Puerto Rican young person." Again, his Health Department released statistics indicating that addiction to heroin had grown by over 70 percent in the years since 1972.[29]

Hernandez Colon, in a typically simplistic explanation, blamed the migration of Puerto Ricans from the United States for the phenomenon, which he called "one of the New York problems." The return of New York-bred Puerto Ricans to the island is, accord-

ing to disturbingly-wide public sentiment, the genesis of many of
these problems, especially crime. But even if there are criminals
and junkies coming from New York and even if some of these
youth learn their bad habits in cities of the United States, something in Puerto Rico must allow such influences to spread. No seed
grows on concrete.

There is an additional fact, again from Hernandez Colon's
Health Department, that in 1977, the first year that this was mea-
sured, the island's hospitals and clinics distributed pain killers
and sedatives to one out of every two patients entering for treatment. While the Department neglected to provide further analysis,
that extraordinarily high statistic seems to indicate that the
problem of drug dependency is greater than originally thought.

Not one of these phenomena—crime, tension, rape and domestic violence, the drugs, or the alcohol—can, in and of itself, be seen
as an indictment of colonialism. "Crime and the problems that
come with it," Mari Bras writes, "are more than present in the
United States, which isn't a colony."[30] But these matters of social
squalor and social decomposition can be taken together to form a
picture of a society which is limping badly and showing the effects
of its increasingly rapid decomposition.

That decomposition only serves to bolster the dependency
created by over-specialization and the destruction of the environment. A society which loses its collective, social cohesiveness logically loses its ability to fight for its independence and just dips
further into dependency. Indeed, that dip into dependency and the
feeling that dependency is the only way to survive for Puerto Rico
have become an essential component of the island's collective
psychology.

The Colonial Consciousness

The old man's address was on a *fichero*, a list of names and
addresses that political parties use for their door to door campaigns. On this Saturday afternoon he welcomed into his house a
young woman from the Puerto Rican Socialist Party, a Marxist
group firmly in support of independence. There was a brief conversation with one of the old man's sons, who politely explained to the
young woman (careful never to look her in the face) that he was
now involved in "religion" and couldn't be involved in politics
anymore. "Religion," the island's term for Pentacostalism, is a

time-consuming undertaking. The young woman turned to the father, "And you, sir, do you consider yourself *independentista?*" "I'm a Popular," the old man said looking at the wall and removing his hat for the conversation.

"What do you think of the situation here in Puerto Rico? Things are bad, aren't they?"

"They're bad all over," he shrugged.

"But they're worse here, right?" she insisted.

Finally he turned to stare at her. "They're bad but there's no way out," he said, shaking his head. "I don't think much of the Americans but I don't know a Puerto Rican I would trust with this island. We are a lazy people and a small people, not a smart people. We can't do it alone."

If there's anything resembling a popular consensus among Puerto Ricans about the status of their island, that comment summarizes it. That's not to say the consensus is accurate: Puerto Ricans are no dumber or smarter, lazier or more industrious, than any other nationality, and small islands and countries do "do it alone." The old man's remark is based on something within the collective psychology of Puerto Rico which runs much deeper than mere logic.

Unlike the traditional colonies of gun-toting soldiers and military governors, Puerto Rico's modern colonialism is not in place through repression. It's not as if repression does not have a home on the island: the list of "investigations," indictments, arrests, and politically motivated beatings and killings is long. But these outrages are outrages only in the context of the society in which they occur; they are nothing like what goes on in El Salvador, Argentina, Guatemala, or so many other countires in which repression is a daily occurrence. That type of repression just isn't necessary in Puerto Rico.

Modern colonialism in Puerto Rico was constructed with the *support* of the island's working people and continues with their acquiescence. Every four years, 85 percent of the Puerto Rican people vote and all but a few thousand of them vote for a colonial party. While this could change someday, it is, at this point, well-grounded in and supported by several very real aspects of Puerto Rican history and society. For one thing, the Commonwealth of Puerto Rico was the fulcrum of the PPD's reformist program, the only program to truly address working-class needs at the time. Today, even while it stumbles, the Commonwealth remains entrenched in working-class politics at the local level. Over a third of the jobs in Puerto Rico are government jobs, making public sector employment the largest area of employment in the country, larger even than manufacturing.[31] While serving to help hide the defects in the Operation Bootstrap development process, public sector employment also makes large numbers of people dependent on the government for their livelihood and makes their allegiance to political parties as well as the system's continued existence difficult to challenge.

What happened in the town of San German is an excellent example of how this dependence works. In 1980, the previously PPD town voted overwhelmingly for the New Progressive Party, which won the insular elections. San German, which had suffered one of the highest unemployment rates on the island was now pleasantly surprised by an influx of construction projects and research grants: all government financed. "Now your vote is key to how you live," Carmen Sepulveda who lives near the town said. "If your town went for the winner, you can expect to benefit."

Since working-class culture has long revolved around the problem of surviving, with little time for abstract debate, mass patronage serves to make working-class people more involved in electoral politics and more reluctant to break with those politics, and in Puerto Rico, involvement in electoral politics is essentially support for the commonwealth government.

The colonial consensus is deepened by the fact that, while life is tough on the island, most Puerto Ricans think it could be a lot worse and, as scholar Frank Bonilla points out, they are probably right.[32] While the island is caught in economic and social quicksand, its head still protrudes. Its people eat; some don't in Central and South America. Its people have homes; some Mexicans and South Americans can't say that. It has island-wide school, transportation, and electrical and water systems. Such things are rare in the countryside of much of the Americas.

Equally important, Puerto Rico is a modern political electoral democracy, the likes of which are indeed scarce in the contemporary Spanish-speaking world. Its people vote, elect officials and those officials make day-to-day policy within the confines of colonialism.

The fact that those with the most important power over Puerto Rico are in Washington is not immediately perceptible to the average Puerto Rican. So skillful is this colonial design that the areas of jurisdiction that most often touch people's daily lives—roads, police, schools, social service agencies, local laws—are all locally controlled. The more important powers, those held by Washington, affect people in much more subtle ways and their only popular manifestations—currency and postage stamps, for example—are uncommunicative, unassuming, and certainly not menacing.

The isolation from colonialist power makes this a colony that just doesn't feel like one and the government's hold over people is often an exercise in image and perception. What is important is not what the government does as much as what people perceive it as doing and in Puerto Rico, a country where there is no "track record" for independent governments, people have been schooled to believe that limited powers are what the government should be about. They may not be satisfied but, like the old man, they see no real alternatives and things don't seem desperate enough to seek them.

Years of perceiving the world like this has brought to the Puerto Rican collective mentality a feeling of complete inadequacy—the idea that Puerto Ricans just aren't as good as North Americans, that Puerto Rico is so small compared to its powerful northern neighbor.

There is the tendency, for example, to call everything that is big and good "American." The largest coffee plant in the southern hills is called *cafe americano,* the best island beef is *bistec americano,* and, as hard as it is to believe, island eggs, fresh and pure of contaminants, are scorned by storeowners for *juevos del norte,* produced in Florida and filled with the chemical and hormone impurities of mass production. There's the desire to attend U.S. schools, the urge to go to the United States, and the collectively-mimicked fashions seen in U.S. magazines that show the wares on blond North American models.

Even the values of North American and European society are inherited. For example, the darker one's skin in Puerto Rico, the less worthy one is considered. In fact, at this late date, most of the island's major politicians are white, a racial minority since the majority is the mulatto racial mixture so typical of creole culture. Many feel that a black person could never win a gubernatorial election in the current Puerto Rico. With such racial intermingling, Puerto Rico is nonetheless victimized by a seldom mentioned but very present racism. While it is more common to see black and brown couples than it is in the United States, it is rare to see black and white couples married or living together. Such marriages are definitely frowned upon.

The society itself is often stratified along racial lines. There are exceptions but, for the most part, professionals are lighter skinned than manual workers. Black Puerto Ricans, for the most part, are involved in the lowest paying jobs, and often live in the worst housing.

The logic behind all this is that people from the United States, in the perception of Puerto Ricans, are white. The whiter you are, the closer you are to being a superior being. There is a pernicious basis to this logic. A country which has never controlled its destiny for one day in its history can hardly make an argument for superiority. In fact, the very concept of success is linked to the United States and its culture and looks, simply because it is the Americans who are not only the successes but who hire the few Puerto Ricans who will be successful.

"The most impressive thing about working in Puerto Rico," says an engineer who went to the island after living in the United States for several years, "is the cooptation and the pressure to become an American. I worked in computers at a bank and, as soon as they realized I had a bit of ability, they tried to force me into management. While doing that, they tried to alter my lifestyle, get me into certain middle-class neighborhoods, get me into socializing with them much more, eating their kind of food, whatever.

"We'd be corralled into these bull sessions late in the afternoon where we'd make fun of the other Puerto Ricans who worked there. I came to feel we were playing this game in front of our bosses to separate ourselves from those Puerto Ricans.

"Well, I didn't want to separate myself from anyone and I just started shying away from the promotions. They made me a shift foreman and that's as far as I went. I found myself almost an outcast and, gradually, they tried to take away all my responsibilities. I was literally forced out because I didn't want to be like them."

It's interesting to contrast the way Puerto Ricans treat Americans on the island with the way people do in Santa Domingo, a much poorer and more repressed country. The average Dominican balks at the kind of bleating subservience Puerto Ricans display when in the presence of an American. An insult by an American will frequently bring shy laughter from the Puerto Rican to whom it was directed.

"I guess you don't speak very clearly, do you," said a young American tourist to an ice cream vendor outside El Moro fort in San Juan. "I asked for vanilla and this doesn't taste like it."

"Maybe vanilla beans down here are taking a nap," her friend quipped and all three, including the vendor, laughed. In Santo Domingo, the ice cream cone would quickly have been an appendage of the woman's nose.

No one is making an argument for the good life in Santo

Domingo, but its relative political independence has apparently made some difference and the Dominicans are well aware of it. They point it out all the time. "Puerto Rico is a tragedy in every way," a Dominican preacher said in 1980, "and the worst thing is the attitude of its people. It's as if they believe they were created a step below everyone else."

These then are the traces of modern colonialism's impact on the Puerto Rican people. An economy which has stagnated and has partly destroyed the environment has created not only the stultifying social problems of crime, social squalor, insanity, and narcotic addiction, but has perverted the collective consciousness.

And colonialism has done one other thing, perhaps its most ugly act. It has arranged, consciously, for the displacement of nearly 40 percent of the Puerto Rican population to another country: the United States.

5

The Journey

One afternoon in the early 1950s, Roberto Sanchez received a gift from the U.S. government: a slice of American cheese and two slices of white bread. "It may not seem like much now," the fifty-eight year old Puerto Rican worker said one day in 1980, "but then it seemed like manna from heaven. I hadn't eaten since I got on the boat."

Sanchez, who has lived on New York's Lower East Side for three decades, remembers picking up the sandwich as he left a medium sized boat after a twelve-dollar, two-day trip from Puerto Rico to the United States. His family had lived for several generations in the countryside near San Juan. Like hundreds of thousands of other agricultural workers, he came to that city looking for the work promised by Operation Bootstrap. "There were some jobs," he said, "but there weren't enough. It was crazy, people jumping all over each other looking for places to stay, for work, willing to do anything. They were selling job applications for thirty dollars each on the street. I told myself this was no way to live and I had to do something."

Twelve dollars on a sure bet was a lot better than 30 dollars for a possibility; so young Sanchez made his decision. He borrowed 200 dollars from his brother, another 150 dollars from a cousin, and about 60 dollars from a few neighbors who had made the journey to San Juan with his family.

"I was ready in March of 1952," he remembered, "and went to my father and told him officially that I was leaving—something he knew I was planning for a while—and asked for his blessing. My father told me to always help people who needed it but not to go overboard because there were many worldly people in New York who did not understand that charity should be repaid. Then he told me that my home was in Puerto Rico and there it would always be and I was to return there when I became wealthy. And he touched my head and bent his own, to keep me from seeing the tears...since men don't like to cry very much...and blessed me. And I was off."

Sanchez made the trip with about 300 compatriots on an old "marine whaler" boat, which tossed and dipped as the undercurrent and waves of the ocean kicked its bottoms and sides. "We slept on the floor, on these mats. I can remember the children crying and the adults praying that we wouldn't sink. But, for most of the two days, people just looked ahead at nothing, ignoring the smell of the vomit. . . We all just sat there quietly and I thought about what was waiting for me...something I couldn't even picture." After the two-day voyage, sandwich in one hand and suitcase in the other, Roberto Sanchez walked out into mid-town Manhattan and stopped to stare. "The first thing that struck me was how big everything was. Where I came from, the biggest thing was the trees and they were maybe fifty feet tall. But there were buildings in New York that one couldn't see the top of...they just kept climbing and I prayed I wouldn't have to go up to the top of those buildings because I knew God would make them fall after a while.

"Then I looked around and realized that I could go to no one. No one on that ship knew where the commonwealth government offices were—no one bothered to give information. The people on that boat just stood there and looked for a long time. We were all alone."

Eventually, all of the voyagers found friends, jobs, and homes in New York, raised families, and created communities which reflected the culture and customs of their homeland. Those communities also suffered some of the same problems as the homeland: unemployment, poverty, and social squalor added to North American discrimination and racism. For most of the voyagers, New York's promise became as false and empty as Operation Bootstrap.

To many North Americans who have shared cities with Puerto Ricans over the last thirty years, these "newcomers" are still a mystery, the "Strangers then Neighbors" of Clarence

Senior's book.[1] Their perceptions have been molded by the racism and colossal ignorance which feed each other.

The history of U.S. cities is, of course, the history of immigration—of people looking for work and a better life. In that sense, the Puerto Rican community is nothing unique. Unlike other immigrant communities, however, this community was fostered by a conscious government policy to create a safety valve for economic problems by exploiting the victims' need to escape those problems. Its creation was an act of colonialism.

The tensions generated by colonialism have made the Puerto Rican immigrant experience additionally unique. The Puerto Rican community is a community sharply divided, filled with conflict between its "first generation"—people born and raised in Puerto Rico—and the "second generation"—those born in the United States.

Jose Luis Gonzalez has called the immigration experience a "central component in Puerto Rican history"[2] and there are few people on the island who do not have relatives living in the United States. For Puerto Rico the impact of the immigration experience has been enormous.

The Policy

"When they brought changes to Puerto Rico, we weren't ready for them and neither were they," Roberto Sanchez said. "I still believe that the government thought it could make all this industry work but, almost immediately, people realized it couldn't."

As Munoz Marin had said of the migration to the United States: "Our problem was there weren't enough jobs for the people and we couldn't bring the jobs in fast enough. Some people had to leave."[3]

The collision between the sudden decline in agriculture and the promised increase in manufacturing brought masses of people to the Puerto Rican cities in a frenzy of job-searching. While the urban-bound migration took a few months, industrialization took more than a decade, during which time factories were opening at a staggered and spasmodic pace. The jobs were not created quickly enough. And even when industrialization was in place, "Bootstrap" never generated the number of jobs eliminated by the death of agriculture. Puerto Rico faced massive unemployment even before its auspicious and controversial experiment got off the ground. Something obviously had to be done.

For decades, Puerto Ricans shared with their Cuban counterparts the dream of going "up North." For the average Puerto
Rican, it was a dream of instantaneous wealth, beautiful homes,
and easy jobs.

With that decades-old illusion festering in the collective consciousness of Puerto Rico, government planners realized that well
organized boat (and then plane) trips and strong publicity campaigns would promote a sizeable migration to New York and,
simultaneously, remove the migrants from the unemployment
rolls.

From 1953 to 1967, 50,000 Puerto Ricans came north every
year.[4] The demographics of migration show just how closely this
migration paralleled industrialization in Puerto Rico. At first,
when light manufacturing dominated the economy, men were the
majority of the immigrants. When heavy industry arrived with
jobs mainly for men, women and children made the trip.

The island government spent about 20 percent of its budget on
this migration.[5] Large billboards advertized the "Job and Home in
New York" slogan. "Marine whaler" boats transported people.
And, in return for tax breaks, businesses provided the government
with names and addresses of people looking for work. In New
York, the government's new "migration" office kept a list of
employers looking for workers and landlords with empty flats and
slum apartments. It matched new arrivals with jobs and homes.
The billboard's promise was in a sense made real.

Based on a percentage of population, this was among the
largest immigrations in history and it was made possible through
the Jones-Shaforth Act which gave Puerto Ricans the freedom to
travel back and forth between the island and the mainland as they
pleased. But the freedom did not spawn any creativity in placement. Migration officials proved less than innovative and, in reality, they had little choice. The immigrants were poor and unedu-
cated people for the most part. And, in their new society, a foreign
language was not a credential but a disadvantage. So workers at
the placement office on 47th Street in Manhattan could have sent
Roberto Sanchez in only one of three directions: to the Brooklyn
Navy Yard where cheap labor was in demand; to the Bronx, where
an impressive development of small factories sprung from postwar industrialism; or to New York's garment center, where needle
trade jobs were being abandoned by the previous generation of
immigrants.

"Depending on where you worked, they found an apartment
for you," Sanchez said. "If you worked in the Bronx or Brooklyn,
you went there and that's how these communities started up. But I

went to the garment district and they sent me to live on the Lower East Side."

Expressed simply, the Puerto Rican community was formed by people moving to areas near their work and where they worked was decided by demands of the market. What underpinned all this was colonialism: the island government created the conditions that forced the migration, constructed the organization to facilitate migration, and set up the mechanism to keep the migrants in their new land.

Reality

As a result of that conscious policy, two million Puerto Ricans (more than 40 percent of the world's Puerto Rican population) live in the United States today.[6] Every major city east of Chicago has a sizeable Puerto Rican community. New York, with over one million Puerto Ricans, is the first and largest. In New Jersey, however, more than a dozen cities have Puerto Rican populations accounting for over 15 percent of the entire citizenry. Migration to those cities was sparked by two simultaneous events: the housing shortage and creeping unemployment in New York.

The heaviest migrations to New Jersey—to the Hudson County area, to southern New Jersey's urban cities, and to Passaic County's cities—began with job openings in those areas and layoffs in New York. When Campbell Soup Company's plants opened in Camden in the late 1950s, for example, the city's Puerto Rican population grew by nearly 60 percent.[7] A reduction in garment center employment in the early 1960s was accompanied by openings in similar jobs in Hudson County's Jersey City and Hoboken. The same was true later in the 1960s of two Passaic county cities: Paterson and Passaic.

In New England, agricultural workers imported to pick lettuce and tobacco have remained in the area, forming younger Puerto Rican communities throughout Massachusetts and Connecticut. An older community in Chicago began with a migration from New York to better paying factory jobs. There are also Puerto Rican populations in Los Angeles and San Francisco, Alaska, Hawaii, and other western states which have formed partly as a result of Puerto Rican soldiers remaining after their tours of military duty.

It is hardly news that Puerto Ricans are poor people. The unemployment rate for Puerto Ricans in this country is over 20 percent (probably much higher when people who have never

worked are counted) and average salaries for a family of four
hover around $10,000 a year. The 1959 salary level was 71 percent
of the national median. Today, it is about 45 percent.[8]

Such economic woes translate to poor living conditions in a
society where housing is a market commodity. According to the
1980 census, Puerto Ricans live in communities where 38 percent
of the housing is "dilapidated" (ready for condemnation). Statistics serve to illustrate a phenomenon the U.S. Commission on
Civil Rights described as "the complete failure of Puerto Ricans to
join the ranks of the upwardly mobile."[9] The census shows that
Puerto Ricans are more isolated than ever before from professional education and jobs, where less than 2 percent of Puerto
Rican men and 5 percent of Puerto Rican women work. True, the
numbers of Puerto Ricans in these jobs have increased, but so have
the overall numbers of Puerto Ricans.[10]

The percentages of Puerto Ricans in the other major classifica-
tions—blue-collar service, blue collar industry, and clerical—have
remained the same for the last twenty years. The only figure which
has grown is the number of Puerto Ricans who do not even bother
looking for work when they turn eighteen. That percentage, now
about 20 percent, has grown by 1000 percent over the last twenty
years.[11]

The Puerto Rican experience exposes the mythological character of "upward mobility." Rather than being a typical experience, upward mobility is a short-lived phenomenon occurring
during the coincidence of some very specific and fairly rare trends.
For example, working-class people move upward appreciably during periods of technological developments which expand industries and create the need for more workers in specific types of jobs.
After World War II, technological developments permitted working-class people to move into skilled and higher paying jobs, since
many immigrants were able to use G.I. Bill benefits to learn one of
the new technical trades (particularly in communications).

But Puerto Ricans came too late. With few factory skills and
no English language ability, they faced real disadvantages in the
job market of that period. In the end, though, the disadvantages
were made to order. Puerto Ricans were not brought here to become
skilled workers; they were brought to remain what they were in
Puerto Rico: cheap labor. As with any cheap labor force, Puerto
Ricans who came to this country filled the spots left vacant by
other immigrants moving on. Those who want to find Puerto
Rican workers need go no farther than a restaurant kitchen in
Boston or Chicago, a factory in Newark, or the Royal Typewriter
Company in Hartford, Connecticut.

In 1970, Royal developed a new office machine. Because there were four times as many requests for machines than Royal could deliver, Royal needed new workers to increase production. Royal looked no further than the Puerto Rican community which was facing a 43 percent unemployment rate at the time. As Royal vice-president Robert Palmer told a 1971 seminar on Puerto Rican labor: "The company's motives—I am not here, of course, to praise the company effort—it was a selfish motive, I want you to understand that."[12] The company hired 421 people, 80 percent Puerto Rican. "Most of these people started on assembly lines," Palmer added. Where did they end up? In ninety days, one-third of them ended up on the streets and only 68 percent of those hired were still working. At the end of the twelve-month period, only seven of the original 421 people were working: all on the assembly line.

Even the types of jobs Puerto Ricans occupy in the United States are reflective of their jobs in Puerto Rico. Assembly line workers, who labored to produce non-durable goods (slightly over 30 percent now) are the heirs to the second stage of industrial development. The small but visible minority who work in heavy industry in the United States are about the same percentage which works in the same industries on the island. Women who work in the garment and other "small shop" industries (comprising over 50 percent of the female labor force) are the heirs of those who operated the sewing machines during Operation Bootstrap's light industry phase. Service workers in the U.S. mirror those who work in the Puerto Rican tourist trade, waiting on tables of rich Americans and shuffling for tips.[13]

Obviously, these types of jobs tend to discourage upward mobility. Industries, like the garment and food trades, are plagued with roller-coaster fortunes at best and an almost unstoppable tendency toward runaway shops or sudden closings at worst. It is difficult to imagine a bus boy in a restaurant or an operator in a garment factory "working their way up" to prosperity though those jobs; in either case, they would be lucky to get a year's steady work. The wages attached to such work linger at the national minimum wage level and for the 60 percent of Puerto Ricans in this category, "saving" money just is not in the cards.

While the economic situation has not changed much, the social situation of Puerto Ricans in this country has changed dramatically. Communities have expanded and become more complex, and while they remain united through self-identification, tensions have developed between different generations. Still, Puerto Rican communities derive their identities from the 63 percent of all U.S.-based Puerto Ricans who were born in Puerto Rico and who are called the "first generation."

The First Generation

The most visually striking thing about a Puerto Rican community is its signs. There are the signs over the grocery stores, giving them their Puerto Rican name, *bodegas*, and identifying them as places where the tropical fruits, vegetables, and products of Puerto Rico are available. These stores are the insurance that Puerto Rican cooking will not become a lost art. There are the signs for social clubs like the *Hijos de Mayaguez*: small clubs of people from the same Puerto Rican town which sponsor softball teams, organize small parties and dances for different occasions, and keep their storefront *locales* open so that people will simply have a place to go. There are the signs for the "ticket agencies" which do brisk business making flight arrangements for people who cannot speak enough English to do it themselves or who are intimidated by the disembodied voice of the airline's sales agent on the other end of the phone.

Not only do such signs identify the community; they symbolize the dynamics underlying the culture of the first generation. *Bodegas* are a central component in the system of community survival. They are important gathering places, as shown by the two young Puerto Rican workers in Jose Luis Gonzalez's short story *"El Pasage,"* who would opt for a *bodega* rather than a neighborhood bar after work. Indeed, bar-owners will attest to the difficulty of starting a neighborhood bar in a Puerto Rican community. Competition from *bodegas* is simply too stiff.[14] But the *bodegero* is not merely a bar-owner. He or she is a community leader and a reservoir of knowledge about the community and the world outside that community.

A great deal of information can be gleaned from the gossip which flows through these stores. For example, Puerto Ricans will often stop in at the *bodega* looking for a relative whose address is not known. An answer, often tinged with gossipy misinformation, is always there. Storeowners also provide information about everything from life insurance to the workings of local government agencies. In this way, the *bodegero* provides a bridge between the community and society in general. Like the church in the U.S. black community, what goes on in a *bodega* reflects the roles community people play and the ways they go about their lives.

During the daytime most customers are women. They stop and talk as long as they like while making leisurely but careful purchases. Women are the keepers of credit with the *bodegero*. During the day, storeowners keep a pile of brown paper bags handy, each of which serves as a credit voucher. No *bodega* survives without a good supply of such bags since credit is essential to its business.

At night, the paper bag vouchers disappear and so, except for the occasional emergency, do most women. *Bodegas* turn into gathering spots of beer-guzzling men who stand in front of the store with beer cans in small bags, talking about everything from sports to local events.

It is as if people packed little sections of Puerto Rico into suitcases, brought them to New York, and opened the suitcase up to lay out the sections. Whole blocks are often inhabited by people from the same Puerto Rican hometown and those people often form hometown clubs which reflect the second characteristic that holds the community together and makes it unique—the dream of returning to Puerto Rico. Most Puerto Ricans born in Puerto Rico will tell you that they want to go back. "I have a piece of land in Puerto Rico," is probably the most common claim made when talk of the island begins. Everyone is always saving up for a little farm on the island. People go back and purchase parcels of land which sit vacant for decades. Sometimes they will return when they hear of an illness or some family emergency. But for the most part, the dream of returning remains only a dream. Too often, the Puerto Rico to which they would return no longer exists; they seem to seek a simpler, crime-free, employing society that is not Puerto Rico today. Yet through the social clubs, community members can still celebrate the Puerto Rico they remember and/or imagine, and they can commiserate in their frustrated dream of return.

In New Jersey, a state with a population of 700,000 Puerto Ricans, there are over 600 such clubs, representing over 40 municipalities of Puerto Rico, according to New Jersey's *Congreso Boricua*.[15] Just as staggering as the number of clubs is their kinetic activity. Besides the obligatory yearly dance for Mother's Day and the gala affair for the day of incorporation of their hometown, the clubs often sponsor softball teams. (There are seventeen hometown leagues in New York City alone, according to the Department of Parks.[16] And they organize contingents in the Puerto Rican Day parades and Puerto Rican Discovery Day celebrations nearest to them.

Moreover, they are a center of nightly activity for men. They rival the *bodegas* as an alternate bar but, unlike the food cluttered stores, they have televisions, pool tables, and other accoutrements in their *locales* (storefronts). "I've worked with these people all my life," says Gilberto Gerena Valentin, whose *Congreso de Pueblos* organized the New York-based hometown clubs into a kind of network in the 1970s. "I'm still surprised when I think of how many of these things there are and how passionate are their members about their hometowns."[17]

Whenever disaster hits Puerto Rico, as it did in 1973 with a rash of floods, the hometown clubs raise tens of thousands of dollars to send to their municipal governments, and clubs are a kind of informal security force in their communities. Whenever someone is in need of help, either after a mugging or because of a car breakdown or some other natural or unnatural disaster, the place to go is the hometown club. They usually have booster cables, a member who is a mechanic, a few strong bodies, a free telephone, a drink, and sometimes a first-aid kit.

Travel

The signs over the ticket agencies also identify one of the means of cultural rejuvenation for this community, something which is more concrete than the dream of returning—the return itself. Many immigrant communities die after the death of their first generations, but that is not the case with the Puerto Rican community because its first generation never dies. While migration has dropped from the 50,000 which arrived in each of the first fifteen years after Operation Bootstrap began, it still continues at a rate of about 20,000 a year.[18] This is a migration figure; it does not count visits back and forth, numbering over 2000 each day.

The migration to the United States injects a daily energy and cultural strength to the community. There is no Puerto Rican born in this country who cannot find a contemporary (no matter what age) among those who arrived last week. Few immigrants enjoy the kind of cultural continuity this perpetual first generation affords.

Constant trips back and forth enhance this cultural continuity. Everyone, no matter where they were born, goes back to Puerto Rico for a visit. The commonwealth government now estimates that half a million Puerto Ricans travel to the island and back every year, making it the most traveled air route in the world. Such frequent travel, possible because the island is a colony and its people are free-travelling citizens, reminds Puerto Ricans of their homeland and revives some feeling of nationality in those born in the United States.

The Second Generation

Living with this first generation, among the signs and trends they symbolize, are 800,000 people born and raised in this country, the "second generation," the sons and daughters of the immigrants. For many years, serious sociologists have alternately described this sector of the community as "assimilated," "victimized by cultural genocide," or "an integral part of the Puerto Rican nation."

Ironically, the three descriptions—poles in what was once a raging debate—reflect the same complicated reality. For what seems like assimilation is really the development of different sets of cultural artifacts and a slightly different world view. What seems like "cultural genocide" is only the interaction between this group of people and the natural forces of the society in which it lives. And the idea of "one nation" is more a simplistic act of faith than an accurate description of reality. Not to say that Puerto Ricans might not be "one nation." In fact, if one asks them, second generation people will respond sharply that they are Puerto Ricans. It might not be clear what that means but the identification is indisputable.

"I do not know why I am what I am, I just am that," a young Puerto Rican woman said at a conference in 1977 at City University of New York. "I'd say it's partly because of my mother and what she talks about and says but it's also because, no matter how good I speak Spanish or not, there's no place else to go...I cannot be nothing else."

The idea of being Puerto Rican starts, of course, with the fact that one's parents are Puerto Rican and they, like virtually every first generation immigrant, have no intention of letting their children forget it. Most of this insistence is unconscious, almost automatic. Parents speak Spanish at home; relatives who live in Puerto Rico are talked about and occasionally called on the phone. Their visits are frequent and often extended.

The Puerto Rican influence is constant and ever-present in the home and vividly reflected on the streets of the Puerto Rican community. The only way to forget one's Puerto Rican heritage would be to move out, like other ethnic second generations have done. But moving out requires money and, because Puerto Ricans are cheap labor, such an option does not exist.

It is true that the 1980 census figures show a slight increase in the number of Puerto Rican professionals and the census profiles indicate that the large majority of these professionals are second generation. But the census also shows stronger increases, almost 10 percent, in the number of Puerto Ricans under twenty not looking for work. And the majority of Puerto Ricans born here are, like their first generation counterparts, still working class, still occupying the same service and low-paying factory jobs, and are still in the same economic straits. The only significant job change between generations is the number of second generation women in the clerical fields who are there as a result of their fluency in English; this is hardly upward mobility. Any change in the status of Puerto Ricans in the United States would require massive educational campaigns and training programs. Figures show that in 1979, more than 70 percent of all Puerto Rican children within the public school system were reading and doing math at a "critically retarded level," three grades below the norm for their age.[19] In New York, for example, 60 percent of Puerto Rican youngsters dropped out of school by age fifteen, the highest percentage of any ethnic or minority population in the United States.[20] "When you teach nothing to a kid," educator Luis Fuentes said, "you're inviting him or her to drop out."[21]

While the reasons for this educational failure are complex, the result is clear: Puerto Ricans are not going to move upward economically, even to the limited extent that is still possible in this society. That means Puerto Ricans will continue to be "ghetto-ized," as James Blaut put it.[22] But the ghetto is not a function of social and economic immobility alone; in the case of minority peoples, it is partly a function of racism.

Racism is an intrinsic part of North American social culture. Even such upwardly mobile Latin Americans as Cuban exiles, who have virtually taken over the economic and political life of a city like Miami, experience the harsh realities of racism. The 125,000 Cubans involved in the 1980 exodus from Mariel harbor, for example, were accused by many white Floridians of "stinking the place up" and "bringing in their diseases."

The racism Puerto Ricans confront isolates them and, in that sense, it is useful to the system that exploits them. The continued use of Puerto Ricans as menial labor is rationalized by the racist conviction that Puerto Ricans can do little else and is most popularly summarized through the saying, "Your accent holds you back." One could not estimate how many times such sentiments are expressed. That most mainland Puerto Ricans do not have accents or that accents are fundamentally irrelevant in most jobs and in most countries is not the point. Racism's logic is to perpetuate a group's position in the labor force, not to be fair. And such exclusion from the economic mainstream is the basis for resistance to assimilation.

Resistance to assimilation co-exists with another strong drive: to separate culturally from the first generation. While the Puerto Rican community's self-replenishing first generation provides a certain cultural and national identity, that identity does not exist in isolation from the rest of the English-speaking world. In most cases, Puerto Rican ghetto communities are near black ghettoes. "I'm not scared to say what I am," Edie Gomez, a Brooklyn-born Puerto Rican high school student said in 1950, "because if you cannot say what you are, you ain't nothing." But what Edie is is not a simple matter. Like most of her mainland-born counterparts, Edie Gomez speaks a mixture of Spanish syntax and English vocabulary sometimes called "Spanglish." It is a strange language: short Spanish phrases thrown in with some English and peppered by the street language of urban blacks.

"If someone calls me out my name, que voy hacer," Edie explained, "Metomano, and then they find out, okay. They come down on me hard and it's a blip, all right. No puedo salir." The last sentence uses "they," a code word for "parents" in Spanish language syntax, and the rest of the sentence just sounds Spanish. The expressions like "blip," "call me out my name," "come down hard," are black English expressions. The vocabulary is mostly English.

Almost every Puerto Rican raised in city ghettoes speaks just like Edie. But these speech patterns were not inherited as a matter of mimicry. For one thing, blacks and Puerto Ricans do not, as a rule, "hang out" together. Indeed, there is often enormous tension between blacks and Hispanics in neighborhoods throughout the country. It is more probable that black English developed as a way of coping with the tensions which confront ghetto people and, since Puerto Ricans confront those same tensions, they have in part adopted a similar use of language.

While Spanglish straddles two cultures, it also pays homage to an articulate street language, based on quickness, economy of phrase, and the implied emotion and nuance of feeling which is central to survival on the streets. Almost without exception, the young Puerto Rican is a ghetto youth, ready to fight, ready to compromise, and wise in the ways of both.

For a white American, the English of Puerto Ricans in this country is virtually indistinguishable from that of urban blacks in the North, especially since Puerto Ricans only use Spanish in the middle of sentences when they are around other Puerto Ricans. The influence is equally evident in mannerisms, forms of dress, and other parts of street culture. And the trappings of black culture are everywhere. "I heard it," for example, is a simple phrase meaning "I understand that what you're saying is deeply felt and you can keep talking" all in one phrase. "I don't be there that much" is a phrase meaning "I do not frequent the place, it is part of my past and I do not think you can reach me there in the future." Black English, as much as some scholars may deny it, is a powerful tool when one must speak quickly and to the point. Even second generation music—disco—is black music that was originally used for a type of Latin dancing. The steps are similar to those of the Cuban *guaguanco*, and the rhythm is black. At many night clubs the two are often mixed. In fact, Latin music is played live at salsa clubs, and disco is played on sound systems between live "sets."

Even salsa, which has declined in popularity among second generation youngsters over the last decade, was intensely affected by classical American black music: jazz. If Ray Barreto can be called one of salsa's premier bandleaders and Eddie Palmieri one of its greatest soloists, both those men must be considered jazz musicians as well. Palmieri played extensively with the late Cal Tjader's jazz ensemble and Barreto worked on dozens of albums with jazz musicians. Even in Puerto Rico, where salsa's purity is supposedly maintained by island bands, the influence has been felt. Papo Lucas, pianist with the Sonora Poncena, the island's oldest band, is actually a jazz pianist who uses all the harmonic and improvisational devices of that form.

The cultural sharing between blacks and second generation Puerto Ricans represents a partial sharing of a world view. Puerto Ricans, like blacks, feel marginalized from the mainstream. They are, in effect, victims of racism and that is how they view themselves. So a North American white is, for a second generation Puerto Rican, a white person. A first generation Puerto Rican would use the island term "North American" or "American"; the term "white people" has an entirely different connotation in Puerto Rico: it means rich people.

It would be misleading, however, to imply that second generation Puerto Ricans are influenced only by black culture and language. Society's transmitters have also affected second generation Puerto Ricans. Television, for example, has influenced young Puerto Ricans through cartoons and television series which often extol the most violent and chauvinistic conceptions of reality. The influence of the TV-cultural norm of U.S. individualism—making it alone is the only way to make it—linked with the reality of the streets has created many changes in Puerto Rican culture.

War-like gangs, unheard of in Puerto Rico, seem to be an outgrowth of the violent ethic of American mass culture which extols the idea of conquest in everything from games to fighting to sex. Most second generation Puerto Ricans do not belong to gangs but equally extreme reactions are reflected in more modest ways. Second generation people are often tough, sharp-edged, and hard. They are street-smart, automatically suspicious, and quick to react. They are urban people; first generation Puerto Ricans are not.

Along with this change from the image of submissive colonized to street-wise tough has been a general withdrawal from religious practice. The New York Catholic Diocese, for example, says that only 7 percent of U.S.-born Puerto Ricans are practicing Catholics, compared to over 40 percent of those born on the island.[23]

"They are unquestionably a different breed, hard to crack and to bring around," Father John Carroll, Diocesan spokesperson in Newark, New Jersey said. "You've got a person who, as a youngster, was exposed to some pretty raw truths in this country's cities and that's not the way I understand things have been in Puerto Rico. At least up to now. So we're dealing with a problem of alienation from the divine will and the acts of God. Someone who asks why God made their friend overdose on heroin is not going to get a very good answer. We do not know and we require blind faith; frequently, it's just not there."[24] And how can it be when, for this second generation, blind faith has so frequently been betrayed?

Of course, there have also been positive cultural changes. American society, for all its barbaric prejudices, still treats women better than island society does, at least in terms of popularly advanced stereotypes. "If you look around, you see women hip," Carlos Sostre, a bus boy in a Manhattan restaurant said. "They can do things as good as guys and you can read how they run businesses and do television shows and write things in papers and magazines. And you know that if their women can do that, your women can do that. So when I get married I ain't saying to the girl:

stay home and cook and raise kids. Because first of all, I know she ain't going to want to do that and plus, together we can do more better than one of us. Which is okay." Never among the second generation would women working be considered immoral, yet among many first generation Puerto Ricans that idea is still prominent.

Despite tensions with blacks, there is also a marked decrease among second generation Puerto Ricans of the virulent racism which characterizes the first generation, probably a result of the street wisdom of the second generation. If racism among minority people has any logic to it at all, it is that the competition for turf, what the Center for Puerto Rican Studies calls "spatial rights," breeds an antagonism which sorely divides people.[25] In this competition, the first generation Puerto Rican is no match for the more experienced urban black but the second generation can hold its own. The equality among blacks and Puerto Ricans serves to make mutual antagonism less prominent.

A unique picture of mainland-born Puerto Ricans has come out of this amalgam of cultural influences. A new myth has been created to rival those of *tainoe* and *jibaro*, portrayed by more than a few writers as quaint and romantic. While poet Jesus Papoleta Melendez offered a vision of the "Nuyorican" as enjoying the absolute best of several worlds, the literary non-conformist Jose Luis Gonzalez stated in 1976 that Spanglish was actually part of the Puerto Rican culture and a rich part at that.[26]

While it is certainly true that quite a few cultural experiences find their way into the young Puerto Rican's life, it is also true that these are revealed in the "ghettoization" Blaut describes.[27] And while it certainly does afford, for the Puerto Rican, a kind of sharing of "a secret language" which automatically defines a national bond, Spanglish is not a language; it is a dialect which lacks the power, vocabulary, and logic of either English and Spanish. This is why most "Nuyoricans" use Spanglish to express their most basic, emotional concepts but when the discussion gets "heavy" they will switch to either English or Spanish and remain there.

Underlying all this confusion is the fact that most second generation Puerto Ricans have little knowledge of Puerto Rican history, customs or, for that matter, the current reality on the island. They are a nationally alienated people, what Maldonado Denis calls "people without criteria."[28]

Blaut, in his defense of the "one nation" thesis, explained that Puerto Ricans became nationalistic because, in part, nationalism always increased during periods of imperialist development.[29] Such analysis was almost *de rigeur* during the period of political muscle flexing by the Puerto Rican independence movement in this country. Just how true it is today depends on how nationalism is defined.

But Blaut makes the important point that whatever confusion exists about Puerto Rican identity would disappear with the demise of colonialism on the island. Perhaps that is why the idea of Puerto Rican independence still attracts such enormous support from Puerto Ricans living in this country, over a third of whom support the independence of Puerto Rico according to a 1978 *Daily News* poll.[30]

Ironically, these same independence supporters are part of the pool of people that includes some of the most disruptive and opportunistic politicians in the Puerto Rican community. Tension within the community can be explained by differences between the two generations, differences which are the basis for the second generation's political role and form one of the most important aspects of the political powerlessness of the Puerto Rican community.

Parallel Power

"Power is a natural thing; its acquisition is a human drive," Stokely Carmichael, the black activist, once said. "And, in oppressed communities, there are both natural and unnatural forms of power developing simultaneously...they compete and the goal of the oppressors is to assure that the unnatural powers win over the natural."[31]

In the Puerto Rican community, two powers have emerged: the power of the selected leaders and the power of the imposed leaders. It is easy to identify the selected leaders. They are a sort of vanguard, a group of people who live the experience of their fellows but, for reasons that are difficult to explain scientifically, become leaders. They are able to understand the needs of these people, express those needs, and communicate them to the power structure.

They are *bodegeros*, for example, who develop a sophistication through interaction with the structure and cunning of the business world while maintaining contact with their own communities. Or they are the men and women who take leadership in a building or a block, through sheer force of personality and vision—

leading rent strikes and carrying community struggles to their logical conclusions. They are community activists, often college educated, who return "home" to pick up on the demands inherent in the needs of their own people, or they are politically involved preachers and priests.

Two things can be said about these leaders: they are respected among their constituents and ignored by everyone outside their constituencies. As the late Evelina Antonetty put it: "The moment the powers that be see you're doing something, they try hard to ignore you. The press ignores you. The politicos try to ignore you and they force you into confrontation so that, when they do cover you, you come out looking like a maniac."

Media ignorance is fueled by the fact that most authentic minority leadership is not elected and that selection runs counter to the normal techniques of identification. Those who do use the more accepted channels are, more often than not, self-appointed leaders. This is where the second generation has played a key role.

The Lost War

It is possible that Lyndon Johnson did not realize what he was doing when he started the War on Poverty. That program, a response to violent riots and obvious social failures, was ostensibly aimed at alleviating societal ills. In fact, the War on Poverty was a program of band-aid solutions. As Richard Nixon would later say, it treated "these problems as if they were isolated: housing as if it were a cold you wake up with in the morning or unemployment as if it were a pulled muscle you suffered at work."[32] Nixon himself realized that poverty was a systemic disorder. To be mitigated, it had to be systematically attacked. Rather than do that, the War on Poverty created a new American phenomenon called "the poverty program."

Anti-poverty agencies cannot be defined by what they did, because each anti-poverty agency concentrated on a specific type of poverty-related problem. Some fought for better housing, some against alcoholism, and some for free medical assistance, legal counseling, or remedial educational programs. Many of them just offered poor and minority kids a place to stay and play during the long, hot summer. It is fashionable now for writers to criticize such programs as "do nothing" exercises, and the results of anti-poverty programs were decidedly mixed. Some were magnificently successful; others were dismal failures.

Because of the image of what Robert Allen calls "the war of cooptation," the most successful anti-poverty programs, like Aspira (the educational organization), disavow any links to the anti-poverty world. But Aspira received federal funds for a decade under the very same laws which funded other, less successful programs.[33]

The problem with these agencies was not that they did not and could not eliminate poverty but that they applied a reformist, band-aid approach to a problem that could only be solved through a complete overhaul of economic and social forces. In the end, the housing they created was quickly overtaken by surrounding blight; rehabilitation projects in the South Bronx and East Harlem were, in a matter of months, rendered useless by graffiti, garbage, and broken windows and doors.

Families did benefit briefly from medical care programs, but diet, living conditions, stress, and general lifestyle remained unchanged. The symptoms were eliminated but not the cause. People still could not afford a better life.

The same was true of drug and alcohol programs which brought temporary improvement to the addict but then returned him or her to desperate streets, prey to the addictive demons. Remedial education did not work because, come September, the students were back in the same schools that developed the problem in the first place. Billions of dollars were invested to make miserable lives a bit easier to live.

Some argue that such an investment was not a bad thing. New York City's anti-poverty program, for example, received about $120 million each year during the decade between 1964 and 1974. "For the money we received at the Bronx Multi-Service Center, we did quite a bit," said Ramon Velez, who is still the principal poverty program emperor in New York's Puerto Rican community. "We received about $12 million a year for this center, which specialized in health care, and we treated about 23,000 people a year...I think that would put us on the level of a major hospital clinic and all of this was absolutely free."[34]

But in order to function, these poverty programs contained regulations requiring that directors, middle managers, and other executives had to come from the small pool of English-proficient Puerto Rican professionals in the major urban centers. "I remember when I went to undergraduate school and would be pretty close with the few other Puerto Ricans in college at that time," Puerto Rican economist Andres Torres said. "And you'd see these people graduate and they would immediately go into poverty programs.

There was not much action during the early 1970s or late 1960s
period for Puerto Ricans in larger companies or other fields: it was
poverty programs."[35]

Poverty programs afforded Puerto Rican professionals and
para-professionals immense employment opportunities. New York
in 1968 was the center for professionals, giving more than 11,000
Puerto Ricans jobs in anti-poverty agencies at executive or middle
management levels. But giving professionals jobs was not the
poverty program's role and this apparent deviation from its stated
goal became the War on Poverty's downfall.

Salaried employees seek to do two things: make a living and
assure the perpetuation of their jobs. The agencies' professionals
toiled at their anti-poverty work with far greater job pressure than
other salaried employees. Since these programs were funded every
year, jobs could end in June with the end of the funding cycle.

"I remember most of our work in the office was keeping tabs on
what we were doing," Hildemar Ortiz, one of the veterans of several such programs, said. "We had to keep exact numbers on who
we saw, what we did with them—everything—and that was in order
to substantiate our work for the new funding application. Then in
January, the whole place would begin writing the new proposal,
and you'd inflate things or make them look a little better than they
were because you were competing with other programs for bucks
and jobs...including your own job. Those programs were a merry-
go-round of funding proposal writing."[36]

Along with the proposal writing would go the required ob-
sequious lobbying of government officials and, in some cases, the
need to apply heavy pressure. There were, during this period,
almost weekly demonstrations at New York's City Hall by organizations seeking funds. The banners spoke of meeting peoples'
needs and even self-determination but the demands were basically
for another year's funding. The end result was that the Puerto
Rican community's most capable professionals, its most charis-
matic and even committed leadership, was reduced to hustling.
And, like the experience in Puerto Rico of the PPD, an entire
generation of leaders was inextricably incorporated into the culture of opportunism.

This opportunism was nurtured by a process of "survival of
the most fundable" through which agency heads without enough
contacts or without the ability to "pad" their proposals just disappeared in the onslaught of poverty program monopolies. In the
South Bronx, Ramon Velez could claim control of over a dozen
different poverty programs. In Brooklyn, former city councilor

Sam Wright could claim control of twice that number. In East Harlem, the Del Toro brothers, Roberto and Angelo, had their own little empire. The lower East Side was divided into four or five kingdoms. By the 1970s, anti-poverty programs were a thriving business, with well delineated turf, and structures which employed hundreds of people. That turf became what Puerto Rican lawyer and politician Herman Badillo called "the minority Tammany Hall."[37]

The poverty programs were para-political structures able to field successful candidates for political office through access to masses of salaried volunteers (the workers in the agencies), money for campaigns, a base of operations, and contacts with the city power structure. And, through rehabilitation programs, they had patronage money for contractors and other businesspeople who could pay their tithe to the political organization during a campaign.

It all paid off. With few exceptions, all the major Puerto Rican political leaders from urban centers have come out of poverty programs, the only real prominent exception being Badillo himself whose political rise pre-dated the programs' development. These leaders often used their political offices to expand and strengthen their poverty programs and to intensify their image as "community leaders." That leadership, however, was based on government funded poverty programs. The new Puerto Rican leadership soon found itself acquiescing to the demands of the government and its officials in order to maintain power and keep the money flowing in.

For example, Velez, a New York city councilor, made the mistake of challenging the Democratic Party by running for Herman Badillo's Congressional seat. Unsubstantiated rumors of mismanagement and extortion resulted in the loss of his Council seat and his funding. Hundreds of second generation Puerto Ricans hired by Velez suffered from his fall from power. All these "poverticians" (another Badillo word) had counted on these second generation professionals, para-professionals, and clerical workers. In many areas, like New Jersey and New England, all the leaders were second generation people.

In a sense, the failure of Puerto Rican politics to build a self-sustaining independence in this country is partly the result of the coopting of second generation political leadership. Like Populism, Puerto Rican second generation politics is, for the most part, an opportunist movement, increasingly virulent and vicious. As things get tougher, the politically powerless cannot resist manipulation.

Gentry

The 1970s saw a decline of many of the industries using Puerto Rican labor. This decline dramatically affected Puerto Rican communities. Confronted by a unionized labor force and inflated costs and overhead, companies picked up shop, as they did in Puerto Rico, and left for less organized pastures in the South and Southwest. They abandoned cities in the southern portion of New Jersey like Perth Amboy and New Brunswick, cities in New York state like Buffalo, towns and cities around Hartford, Connecticut, and, of course, New York City itself.

This industrial flight savaged local economies, causing a drop in tax tables by, for example, almost 30 percent in New Brunswick and forcing massive cuts in social services. Urban planners who had, up to then, specialized in ways to improve city life were faced with a new challenge: saving the cities from bankruptcy. For the first time, officials in cities like Paterson and Newark were faced with a new option: the death of their cities. The emerging urban strategy spelled disaster for Puerto Rican communities. Like the "Bootstrap" planners, these urban planners were faced with the "problem" of poor people taking up apartment and house space which could be occupied by people with higher salaries, people who would pay higher taxes.

"Cities in major metropolitan areas, like the New York metropolitan area, have something unique to offer," urban planner and former Passaic City Business Administrator Kenneth Mahony once said during an interview. "They can offer amenities, cosmopolitan life, and centers of enormous job opportunities for professionals. Where can a lawyer, a public relations expert, a doctor, or some other professional find more work opportunities than in New York and there are several middle-sized urban cities within a half hour of New York." In Hartford, Connecticut, over 11,000 Puerto Ricans were displaced when over twenty blocks along the city's main thoroughfare were torn down within three months in 1973 to make way for condominium and commercial buildings. In Hoboken and Jersey City, New Jersey, condominium developers, seeking to take advantage of the inflated apartment costs in nearby New York, helped destroy around 40 percent of Puerto Rican housing stock. Jersey City reduced its Puerto Rican population by 50 percent and Hoboken got rid of over 14,000 Puerto Ricans within three years.

In New York's Park Slope, one of Brooklyn's major Puerto Rican communities during the 1950s and 1960s, affordable brownstones became the homes of professionals who took over from absentee landlords, rehabilitated, and moved right in. Park Slope has lost 70 percent of its Puerto Rican population within the last ten years.

Several factors eased this process of gentrification. Puerto Rican residents did not usually own their own homes. "Gentrifiers" (professional home seekers) would buy one- or two-family houses from an absentee landlord and the renters, unprotected by city laws, had to move out. Often, those gentrifiers would raise the income level of their investment by "puffing up the neighborhood" to other potential buyers, who would then pay extremely high purchase prices, rehabilitating the homes for "young urban professionals." Finally, while the neighborhood was "turning" (non-Puerto Ricans moving in), few Puerto Rican owners could resist making a 300 percent profit on their original investment. In other cases, absentee landlords would hire someone to burn their buildings so they could sell the land to a developer, collect the insurance, and get rid of the headaches which accompany a ghetto property.

After a short time, living in these communities becomes uncomfortable for Puerto Ricans who are blamed when the crime rate invariably goes up as drug addicts and other street hustlers take advantage of the new residents who have more affluence than street smarts. Police begin chasing Puerto Ricans off the streets which they have traditionally used as recreation areas. Local *bodegas* close for lack of business or because they are bought out by "boutique" shops. The new children on the block snub Puerto Rican kids, and speak and think differently than Puerto Rican kids. They are forced to relocate, searching their new country like nomadic tribes for a decent place to live and a decent job. And their political power is even further disrupted by the instability of their community. Their experience is an indictment of colonialism. Operation Bootstrap offered them a job and a home but after three decades they have neither.

6

Old Crises, New Politics

The Unravelled Consensus

The Popular Democratic Party (PPD) ran Puerto Rico's government virtually unchallenged between 1948 and 1968. During those two decades, the PPD not only established what scholar Arturo Morales Carrion calls "the deepest possible popular consensus"[1] in favor of the Commonwealth but it succeeded in making itself the popularly accepted symbol of that consensus.

What was once offered by the PPD and viewed by many of its supporters as a transitional status in preparation for independence evolved during those two decades into a seldom-challenged reality. So deeply ingrained was that consensus in the political culture of the country that an electoral challenge to the PPD was treated as an act of folly or buffoonery.

And the father figure of the PPD, Luis Munoz Marin, became a demigod. An entire generation of Puerto Ricans grew to the age of social and civic responsibility under his governorship. They knew nothing else; for them, Munoz Marin *was* Puerto Rican government.

Such power over the hearts and minds of the people came partly through the careful construction of a mega-leader mystique, something Munoz Marin was highly skilled at. And a certain political inertia does sometimes set in when a person has been

117

governor for as long as most people can remember. But the consensus was built on much more than that. Because the *Populares*
governed Puerto Rico during its modernization, they were not only
able to take credit for the resulting advances in Puerto Rico, but
the modernization gave the PPD control over everything—from
decisions on corporate tax benefits and government business
loans to who held which job. Soon any decision the government
made about a person's life was made by an activist of the PPD. In
short, the PPD brought to Puerto Rico a patronage system which
continues to be unrivalled by that of any American city. It became
a fact of Puerto Rican life that support for the *Populares* was the
key to economic survival.

Partly to feed this increasingly voracious patronage system
and partly as a means of masking the fundamental failures of
Operation Bootstrap, the government hired more and more employees, creating more and more civil service and government-
paid positions. The number of workers in civil and public employment positions rose from 14 percent in 1954 to over 35 percent
fourteen years later and, by 1968, Puerto Rico's government had
become its principal employer. It's not hard to see why Puerto
Rican workers voted loyally for the PPD and religiously mouthed
support for the Commonwealth; most of them owed the Commonwealth and the PPD their jobs.

But a consensus built on such shaky ground was bound to
unravel and, by 1968, that was clearly happening. Puerto Rico's
economy—the lynchpin of PPD hegemony—was collapsing, the
victim of the same combined tendencies of inflation and economic
shrinkage that produced the already percolating economic crisis
in the United States. (Although in the United States, the crisis was
partially masked by the Vietnam War.) Puerto Rico's economy
was, of course, intricately linked to the colonial power and the lashes
of the mainland crisis were felt even more painfully on the island.
During the late 1960s, the island was hit by a rash of small plant
closings that virtually eliminated the already paltry group of
island-based small industries that had survived the debacle of
Operation Bootstrap. Unemployment on the island increased by 3
percent a year between 1968 and 1972 and over 60 percent of those
unemployed were industrial workers.

The economic crisis turned the economic dream scenario—the
basis of the PPD's appeal—into a nightmarish joke and the people
most hurt by the joke were the small Puerto Rican capitalists and
the industrial working class. The weakening of two of the PPD's
most important groups of constituents brought a significant
threat to the PPD's support base.

Of course, the crisis also brought problems to the traditionally non-PPD sectors like the larger Puerto Rican businesses who survived mainly through service to large U.S. firms. As the U.S. firms sought to soothe their own suffering by cutting back on island operations, these Puerto Rican service businesses—construction and machine parts businesses, for the most part—saw their fortunes stagnate. As their financial losses increased, so did their opposition to the PPD and their resolve to finally withdraw their support altogether.

In politics, crisis always leads to political challenge and, in 1968, that is just what happened in Puerto Rico. The challenges came from many fronts—the ballot box, the university campus, and the factory gate. And the challenges, like the crisis itself, were not only to the confused and battered PPD leadership but to the very status of Commonwealth itself.

Puerto Rican politics would never again be the same.

More False Promises

If one word could describe how these economic problems and the resulting unravelling of the consensus were reflected in electoral politics, it would be "instability." It is safe to say that today no political party holds hegemony over the electorate. Rather, the popular will seems to shift between two parties—the PPD and the New Progressive Party (PNP), the party that favors statehood for Puerto Rico.

To wit, in 1968, the newly-organized PNP elected construction magnate Luis Ferre to the gubernatorial post. He was unseated in 1972 by a lawyer and PPD bureaucrat named Rafael Hernandez Colon, who lost the governorship in 1976 to another lawyer, this time from the PNP—Carlos Romero Barcelo. Romero Barcelo was re-elected to the post for a second term in 1980 and some commentators hinted that a return was in the offing to the days of hegemonic one-man rule. But those pundits' predictions proved premature—Romero Barcelo was dumped in 1984 by none other than Rafael Hernandez Colon who miraculously rose from his political grave to win that election.

Trying to make anything of the flip-flops in Puerto Rican politics is to waste time diving into the insignificant daily travails of island politics; very little of interest is revealed. Ferre won the governorship in 1968 from Roberto Sanchez Villela, a liberal reformer who was Munoz Marin's hand-picked successor but later alienated the Populist godfather (and many PPD organizers) by trying to force land and small business reforms. Ferre then lost in 1972 largely because he proved to be among the most inept campaigners in island history and because Luis Munoz Marin came out of retirement to campaign for Rafael Hernandez Colon. Hernandez Colon in turn lost because he proved an inept and bumbling bureaucrat. And Romero Barcelo lost in 1984 because of his connection to a corrupt police administration that was implicated and later indicted in the scandalous murder of two young *independentistas* a year before.

That's what makes governments in today's Puerto Rico and it is a sign of degeneration. This, after all, is an island which followed a PPD with ideas and a concept of the future, with a platform and a politically holistic approach. Unfortunately, that program led the island into a colonial quagmire in which no party can realistically pose any meaningful reform. And so the electorate waffles, swayed by short-lived scandals and superficial impressions and the electoral politics of Puerto Rico gyrate in a grotesque dance of meaninglessness.

Evidence of such political ineffectuality and meaninglessness is readily available in the PPD's recent history. While the PNP has offered its new alternative—statehood—the PPD has tried to change the appearance of its old one. In fact, almost all of the PPD's efforts and activities have revolved around the development of a series of "new proposals" which do little more than re-phrase the concept of Commonwealth. In 1974, for example, Governor Hernandez Colon tried to get the U.S. Congress to support something he called a "new compact" between the mainland and island governments. The proposal did redefine some American rights and privileges on the island and stretched Puerto Rico's jurisdiction over water rights. The proposals were of a totally legalistic nature—defining the responsibilities of the Puerto Rican government in administrating the colony. They never really challenged the concept of colonialism itself. Still Hernandez Colon took the idea seriously and his resident commissioner, Jaime Benitez, spent the entire year scurrying about Capitol Hill trying to drum up Congressional support. Because the "new compact" idea did little for U.S. economic and political needs, Congress did to Benitez what it has often done with Puerto Rican government initiatives—it simply paid no attention.

With each election, there is a new idea—a new constitutional convention, a "transfer of powers" which (unlike the *independen-*

tista version of the concept) dwells on administrative rather than real power or, in the most recent case, a "government without corruption" which somehow will attract more American investment into the country. Facile, superficial non-solutions put together in platforms that only serve to unmask the difficult and perplexing truth—the Commonwealth system is dead. It played a historical role in the development of Puerto Rico and now it has no further role.

New Alternative

Perhaps the only significant electoral-political development of the last several decades has been the rise of the New Progressive Party. A right-wing organization with ties to the mainland's GOP that supports the idea that Puerto Rico should become the fifty-first state, the PNP is conservative, strongly anti-union, and vehemently anti-communist. It is also something of an enigma, a grouping of very strange bedfellows. Its ranks include intellectuals like Juan Manuel Garcia Passalacqua and political operatives like Franklin Delano Lopez and Baltazar Corrado. It has attracted industrialists like Ferre himself and many federal court lawyers, like Romero Barcelo, who are perjoratively referred to by their peers as "the American boys"—trained as lawyers in the United States and capable of practicing law in English, the language of the Federal courts in Puerto Rico. While it might seem surprising that sophisticated politicians like Corrado del Rio and brilliant (if cynical) intellectuals like Garcia Passalacqua could collaborate with political primitives like Ferre or Romero Barcelo, there is a basis for collaboration that makes the PNP both significant and, to many, very dangerous.

The "new intellectuals," industrialists, and politicians of the new PNP shared a concern about the situation on the island: the increasing activity among university students demanding reforms, the constant strikes and the flowering of the independence movement, and corporate flight and the difficulties in recruiting new business to the island. Out of these concerns, the fulcrum of the PNP platform was developed: statehood for Puerto Rico. In that one slogan, the PNP took on its opponents with a sophisticated alternative. Statehood, PNP leaders explained, was not a plot hatched in Washington nor did it require a surrender of the island's character and distinctiveness. Indeed, statehood was a right which the United States has actually been denying Puerto Rico.

While Ferre first posed the demand for Puerto Rican statehood, Romero Barcelo made this once laughable option into an acceptable possibility for the island's people. "We will not rest," said a militant Romero Barcelo in 1976, "until there are fifty-one stars on the American flag."[2] Although Romero himself admitted shortly after the 1980 election, "No majority exists in favor of statehood," the PNP still showed it could win elections. While many PNP supporters were not proponents of statehood, they at least did not consider it to be the anathema that it had been during the 1950s and 1960s.

The PNP advanced the statehood concept the same way the Commonwealth alternative was framed in the 1940s—as an anti-colonialist demand. "Puerto Rico is a colony whose people have the obligations but not the powers of citizens of the United States," Romero said in 1977. "They cry out for this right and our goal is to see that we achieve it."[3] In short, the PNP—whose leaders freely use previously taboo terms like "colony"—has relied on the fact that something has to be done. "If we continue like this much longer," PNP leader Franklin Delano Lopez said, "we'll be unable to choose any alternative because this island will be worth very little. Everything, from the economy to the society at large, is in very bad shape.[4]

According to the PNP's publicly described scenario, statehood would be achieved through a referendum vote mandating the Puerto Rican government to carry the message to Washington. The messenger would be the island's representative to Congress, called the "Resident Commissioner," who has certain rights and privileges, including sitting on and participating in committees but who has no voting rights or power to propose legislation. This Resident Commissioner would find some lawmaker to draft a bill for statehood to be put before Congress which would then vote to make Puerto Rico the fifty-first state in the union.

As controversial and passion-provoking as this scenario is, it is hardly absurd. Since Puerto Rico's government is already patterned after that of a state, little rearrangement would be necessary. And, despite anti-statehooders' claims that the Puerto Rican economy would suffer and its culture be assimilated, there is no evidence that either would occur. Indeed, pro-statehood Presidents like Gerald Ford (who proposed an ill-fated statehood bill during his lame-duck incumbency) insisted that the Puerto Rican language would remain the same. Additionally, Puerto Rico's "Commonwealth" economy is so closely connected to the United States that statehood would probably not change it significantly.

On the other hand, pro-statehooders' claims that the island would benefit economically and politically after statehood are ridiculous. Puerto Rico is already getting more federal aid than most states. It is true that with statehood Congressional representation would increase and people could vote for the U.S. President, but in such a large Congress, a Puerto Rican delegation would have little impact. Nonetheless, the PNP has been able to present its platform as a viable alternative for the Puerto Rican people. "There are two reasons for Puerto Rico to be a state: commonwealth and independence," Romero said. "Commonwealth status is bankrupt, that's obvious to everyone. Colonialism does not work. Independence is an alternative to colonialism, but, let's face it, it does not have popular support and the reason is that for an island as small as ours, independence is folly. No small country can exist without links to others, real firm links, and our people would certainly be better off linked to the United States, with full rights, than to any other country. History in Puerto Rico is already a history of relationships with the United States."[5]

While statehood would yield little for the average person, some Puerto Rican industrialists and bankers believe that it would at least put them on some kind of parity with U.S. companies. While U.S. companies would still gain tax benefits, those same benefits would also have to apply to Puerto Rican-owned businesses. Statehood would also eradicate the enormous trade restrictions on Puerto Rican businesses allowing them to trade with any U.S. trading partner.

It would be a mistake, however, to view the PNP's ascendancy the mere outgrowth of industrialist support because, if demographics are any indication, the PNP's industrial and blue-collar base is now larger than that of the *Populares*.

In part, one can interpret this increase in working-class support for the PNP as a repudiation of PPD policies, particularly those affecting unions. For not only has the PPD been unable to resolve the island's economic problems, a logical and consuming concern of industrial workers, but it has consistently and unrelentingly opposed unions and viciously attacked organized labor activities. This is particularly true with respect to civil service workers, who are forbidden from organizing under island laws promulgated and defended by the PPD.

Yet, the pro-PNP trend still dramatizes a shift in working-class perspective towards statehood. Even though support of the

PNP does not reflect a pro-statehood sentiment, as PNP leaders are themselves quick to admit, the fact remains that these workers are voting for a party whose platform would have been a political impossibility in the past. They have finally accepted the concept of statehood as a viable, if not an advantageous, alternative. What is most important about the rise of the PNP, then, isn't its electoral success—because it loses as many elections as it wins—but that it can legitimately participate in those elections with its platform.

In one sense, the PNP's rise seems to be little more than an updated version of the traditional illusion that the United States is key to the island's survival. But there is a degree to which such a concern reflects reality. Economically, Puerto Rico has gone from being an imperfect microcosm of the U.S. economy to being a center for very specific industries. Industrial specialization has made Puerto Rico almost the equivalent of a state, sporting the "one-or-two-industry" label delegates to political conventions wear on their lapels. Puerto Rico could be the "pharmaceutical state," for example.

These changes in the economic structure of the island are accompanied by apparent changes in the strategic use Washington is making of Puerto Rico. Military presence, of course, has been the one constant since the United States took over Puerto Rico. As can be expected in any colony, however, the role of those bases changed as the military policies of the United States changed. During the world wars, they were stationing and basic training facilities for U.S. troops. During Korea and Vietnam, when recruitment from Puerto Rico itself was high, they were home to the Puerto Rican soldiers and provided military beach front areas on which to practice new invasionary techniques.

Puerto Rico may have always been militarily useful, but over the last ten years it has become militarily crucial and that is because there has been a shift in U.S. military attention from Southeast Asia to Latin America and the Caribbean. Under President Reagan, Washington has developed one of the most aggressively militaristic policies in this hemisphere in history. There is, of course, a long history of covert action against revolutionary movements and progressive governments in Latin America and the Caribbean and there is some history of direct invasion, as is the case with the Dominican Republic in 1965, but never has the U.S. government so brazenly carried on so many battles in so many countries simultaneously. The unprecedented militarization of the island is a direct result of this policy.

Today, in Puerto Rico and Vieques (a small satellite island-municipality), there are over twenty active military installations; they literally form a string around the entire island and cover about 75 percent of Vieques' land. The bases are part of a still-current Pentagon program to expand the military use of Puerto Rico.

While expansion of the facilities is important in and of itself, what is more important is the transformation of Puerto Rico into the principal military base in Latin America. Not only is it a training facility for "marine-to-land counter-insurgency" but it is now apparently the principal staging point for such missions. Carlos Zenon, the president of Vieques Fishermen's Association calls his island "a military bridge between the United States and the rest of the hemisphere." The bridge was used during the Grenada invasion, for example, which was rehearsed in Vieques two years before it occurred. When the invasion order was finally given in 1983, U.S. troops actually embarked from staging points on Vieques beaches. The same is true for almost all the many incursions by U.S. warships into Nicaraguan waters.

The situation provokes many concerns among environmentalists and activists. Because of the increase in the military use of Puerto Rico, the United States has increased its storage of high-tech weaponry in the western section of the island. No one is sure just what this weaponry is—some activists insist that a portion of it is nuclear, though the island government denies it and the Pentagon never comments. But, nuclear or not, the bombs stored in the facilities which blanket large sections of the less populated western side of the island represent a real threat to the physical security of the island.

At this point, there is no telling whether the U.S. government would favor a statehood solution or whether statehood could help an island which is emptying and abandoning its factories and turning into a military base. It is obvious, however, that Puerto Rico is rapidly approaching the stage when its residents are superfluous to U.S. interests, when residents are encouraged to leave, and when many of those who stay are supported marginally by federal programs.

If anything, President Reagan's recently unveiled plans for the Caribbean, called the Caribbean Basin Initiative, seem to point to this "empty island" approach. The Initiative seeks to eliminate most of the tariffs on products coming into the United States from Caribbean countries *other* than Puerto Rico. Tariffs have not traditionally applied to Puerto Rican-made goods because goods coming from other markets (like the Virgin Islands) are more cheaply made and priced. To give Puerto Rico an edge and make the island competitive, the United States has taxed other basin products at up to 65 percent of their prices; clearly favoring American businesses who were finishing products in Puerto Rico and sending them to the United States. The possibility of eliminating this edge was shock to both PPD and PNP officials. The scheme, essentially, would promote the movement of U.S. industries out of Puerto Rico and to other countries.

"Indigenous Caribbean products will replace Puerto Rican products in the mainland markets and, more important, in Puerto Rican markets," House Speaker and PPD leader Severo Colberg said. "American firms will be encouraged to move their labor intensive Puerto Rican operations to low-wage Caribbean countries. Finally, products from Puerto Rico will be placed in direct competition with Japanese and European products...Eventually, unable to export its products, Puerto Rico will be forced to export its most valuable resource: its people." Hence the "empty island."[6]

While the Puerto Rican population decreased during Operation Bootstrap, an "empty island" period would show much larger migrations. Operation Bootstrap maintained a 25 percent unemployment rate; today 40 percent are unemployed, and cutting food stamps and other social benefits would swell those numbers, leaving people without any means of subsistence.

Immigrating to the United States, however risky, would look like an ever more attractive option. Is it possible that the island could actually be emptied? Because of life-threatening economic conditions in Mexico, over 800,000' people illegally cross the southern border into the United States each year. If similar conditions prevailed in Puerto Rico, how many people would migrate legally? While it is not probable that the island would literally empty, it *is* conceivable that about 300,000 industrial workers would move, virtually eliminating the island's most stable sector and a good part of the labor movement's membership. Such an occurence would obviously weaken labor and popular movements, making them less resistant to cultural and economic repression. It would also dash the hopes for an independent economy, since it would take away the class on which such an economy would be based. Most of all, it would necessitate changes in the island's political structure. The Commonwealth is now and has always been a kind of service agency for the island's working class and an administrator of its labor force. Much of its bureaucracy is designed to smooth relations between U.S. companies and Puerto Rican workers. When tensions can't be resolved using bureaucratic measures, the island police are always on hand. A massive exodus of workers would make this function and its corresponding government bureaucracy superfluous.

Independentism

In its section on Puerto Rico, the Amoco Tourist Guide to the Caribbean describes a "large independence movement seeking separation from the United States."[7]

One can almost picture the guide's readers doing a double-take. After all, Americans have been told for decades that the independence movement is not a political force at all. Opponents of Puerto Rican independence have long pointed out that, since World War II, independence parties have routinely suffered spectacular defeats during elections. Never has any pro-independence party—including the social democratic Puerto Rican Independence Party and the Marxist Puerto Rican Socialist Party—garnered more that a 10 percent share of the vote. As PPD leader Miguel Hernandez Agosto told the United Nations in 1977, "They may argue all they want but the polls show the *independentistas* have no popular suport."[8]

Hernandez Agosto was, however, one speaker on a list of over forty that year which included *independentistas* representing organizations like the Puerto Rican Bar Association, the Institute on Culture, the Free-Masons, and several environmentalist organizations, women's groups, and labor organizations as well as twelve different political organizations besides the PIP and the PSP. The combined membership of those organizations was over 120,000. There was probably much overlap but probably just as much sympathy not reflected in the membership numbers. The fact is you can't gauge the influence and impact of an opposition movement with election results.

Just what is the independence movement?

The independence movement can best be understood as an opposition movement with all the complex relationships, myriad outlets, issue-specific committees and organizations, and political parties that characterize similar movements in any industrialized society. And, like any such movement, its influence reaches far beyond its organizational structures. In Puerto Rico, *independentistas* individually play leadership roles in virtually every area of contemporary popular concern and activity.

In the electoral circus, with its bombardment of advertising
and media manipulation, colonialism still reigns. Despite that
hegemony, however, independentism has been instrumental in
defining both the cultural and educational life of the island since
most of Puerto Rico's important artists and writers, as well as its
most prestigious scholars, are publicly in favor of independence.

Despite the obvious support of the PNP among industrial
workers, the independence movement has been the most important political force within the country's contemporary labor
movement; the most militant labor leaders are all *independentistas*.

Finally, in the areas like environmental protection and quality of life, where the colonial government exercises administrative
power, the movement for independence has been the principal
brake on policies which would destroy the resources of the country
and make it physically unable to be independent. "Were it not for
the movement," scientist Neftalie Garcia explained, "Puerto Rico
would be much farther advanced toward its own destruction."

Like any opposition movement, independentism is made up of
smaller struggles seeking short-term objectives that are harmon-
ious with independentism's long-range goals. The logic for *independentistas* has always been the same: preserve those aspects of
culture, environment, and economic life which are central to the
survival of Puerto Rico and are potential areas of recruitment to
the movement. While it would be a mistake to view all struggles
around economic, environmental, or cultural issues as pro-independence, they are almost always led by *independentistas* and they
are always supported by the independence movement. In fact,
these struggles more than anything else have provided the movement with the vitality and sense of spontaneity that make it
colonialism's most worthy adversary.

For example, on more than one occasion the island government has sought to sell to U.S. corporations the right to strip-mine
the middle portion of Puerto Rico. On each of these occasions, the
independence movement has exposed the unpublicized secret contracts and successfully mobilized public opinion against them. In
each case, the contracts have gone unsigned.

The same has been true of government attempts to bargain
away portions of Puerto Rico's water rights and attempts to
change the island constitution to restrict political activities.

It was true of the battle over the beaches in the early 1970s,
during which hundreds of young people walked onto hotel-owned
beaches previously off-limits to Puerto Ricans and sat down in a

version of civil-rights sit-in tactics. Today, insular law makes all beaches public. Even though hotels and private apartment buildings do everything from installing security doors to ten-foot high fences to keep people out, anybody who can get to a beach cannot be removed from it.

And it was equally true of the massive electricity boycott of the mid-1970s during which thousands of people refused to pay their electricity bill. Those whose electrical service was turned off for non-payment could call one of the many *independentista* activists from the electrical workers union who would visit that evening and restore service. These popular struggles against policies that attack the resources of the island or make living there more difficult are vital to independentism. Obviously, it is in the interest of pro-independence forces to protect the natural resources of the country and keep its people on island soil.

During particular periods in recent Puerto Rican history, these battles have thrust the independence movement into a prominence that the mere agitation for a change in status could never offer. They have made independence the principal opposition to the government, more important and more active than any other opposition force. As Governor Hernandez-Colon once said, "Everything we do here is going to be opposed by the *independentistas*. They are this country's main problem."

Ironically, the *Populares* have played a major role in the development of the pro-independence movement. While independentism has been a political force in Puerto Rico since the 1800s, the modern independence movement is very much a product of the monumental changes in the economy and the political and social trends that have developed in Puerto Rico. In fact, the movement is premised on the idea that Puerto Rico is headed for a colonial crisis that will inevitably make independence the only realistic alternative. This projection has been the strategic underpinning of independentism since the early 1960s. In fact, such a perspective would not have made much sense before the rise of PPD, the Commonwealth, and Operation Bootstrap since these developments served to entrench colonialism and finally mire it in chronic crisis.

Predictably, three of the areas where the modernization of Puerto Rico has been most pronounced—the university, the economy, and the popular arts—are the three areas where pro-independence thought and leadership has had the most impact.

The Student Movement

The almost complete smashing of the Nationalist Party, and the incorporation of the island's new industrial workers into the ranks of the PPD's support, gave the *Populares* virtual freedom to do what they wanted with Puerto Rico's economy and governmental structure. While it busily built up its infrastructure of roads and support services, simultaneously fine-tuning the administrative laws necessary to Operation Bootstrap's continuation, the government was also modernizing an important component of its superstructure: the university system.

Like many Latin American university systems, Puerto Rico's had been steeped in the traditional function of higher education: taking the island's "rich and well-born" and, as Alexander Hamilton would have it, making them "able." It was principally a liberal arts system whose schools concentrated on training its upper-class students to be lawyers and doctors.

By the late 1960s, however, the role of the university was rapidly changing. The University of Puerto Rico was beginning to create "branches" in other parts of the island dedicated to the development of professionals who would become the island's expanding management sector. New schools in engineering and economics were already functioning in Mayaguez and at the central campus in Rio Piedras, and the law school had expanded to include specializations in government and corporate law.

The expansion meant an increase in the size, shape, and variety of the student body. As the demand for professionals surpassed the ranks of the island's gifted, well-born and able, thousands of working-class youngsters found admission to the university easier. There were government grants and scholarships for students, expanded programs of fund-raising and direct government funding for the university, and a more intense recruitment policy at the public high school level.

Such an expansion was bound to have liabilities. The opening of the campus brought young people whose experience differed widely from that of the sons and daughters of the affluent and they were quickly immersed in a system which had become a center for political struggle where students routinely studied the literature of third world thinkers, Cuban writers, and Marxist intellectuals.

Furthermore, there was a war going on in Vietnam and an international movement of young people had risen to vigorously oppose it. Intellectually, the increasingly radical students found themselves in solidarity with the Vietnamese and, emotionally, they found themselves in fear of and resentful of the draft of Puerto Rican students. After all, the last thing these working-class youngsters wanted was to be plucked from Puerto Rico, replete with unprecedented opportunities for them, and be sent to fight in a war that most of them already found repugnant and that was being waged by a power they deeply resented.

The draft provided the first massive issue of the post-Nationalist independence movement and yielded the first truly massive university demonstrations in history. The anti-draft movement on campus routinely mobilized thousands of students. In September of 1968, a young activist named Edwin Feliciano Grafals borrowed a tactic from the U.S. Civil Rights movement and activist Rosa Parks's refusal to sit in the back of the bus; he refused to cross the line when his time for selective service recruitment came. Feliciano was arrested, tried, and sentenced to one hour in prison and, as the movement of which he was a leader expected, the university became a battle-ground.

The percolating opposition to the draft spilled over and since they couldn't march on the White House, the students found the next best target—the ROTC building on campus. A two story structure that housed the ROTC offices and the residences of many of its cadets, the building proved an outstanding target and the cadets acquitted themselves marvelously as foils. These students constituted some of the most right-wing on the campus: almost all pro-statehood, rabidly anti-left, and militantly anti-independence. They spouted the right-wing rhetoric of law and order and free enterprise, of the fight against communism and the imperial glory of the United States: the watchwords of American conservatism. They often walked through the campus cafeteria behind the American flag (it is considered an insult in Puerto Rico to fly the American flag without the Puerto Rican flag next to it), wore little flag lapel buttons, and even spoke to each other in halting English.

Because they were, indirectly, part of the U.S. military, because they deferred to U.S. presence both in Puerto Rico and in Vietnam so willingly, and because they were virulently anti-independence, the ROTC students made a wonderful symbol. The target was there; the battle was on.

During that first semester the fight to abolish the ROTC became the most important issue on the campus. There were weekly demonstrations, pickets in front of ROTC buildings, and constant attempts to disrupt the ROTC practice sessions. Predictably, the ROTC students continued what had become an escalating battle between themselves and the *independentistas*. There was frequent fighting, constant heckling and escalating polarization on the campus.

Things came to a head when, in 1968, the Academic Council, made up of university professors, responded to student pressure by voting to abolish the ROTC. The action gave the island government an excuse to intervene and Ferre, just elected, was more than happy to do so. He recognized the campus as the center of the period's pro-independence thought. Putting things in order there became his law and order priority. "University is for study," he said, "not for demonstrations and subversive ideas."[9]

Certain that some of those subversive ideas were coming from professors, Ferre had already placed the entire unviersity hierarchy under a governing council made up of gubernatorially appointed "citizens." The patronage-packed governing council was two weeks old when the professors decided to abolish the ROTC. "It was," "Maldonado Denis, a professor at the University, writes, "a made to order confrontation situation."[10]

The citizens' council did the predictable: it overturned the Academic Council decision and, killing two birds with one stone, it fired the Rio Piedras campus (which was the most polarized campus) reform-oriented chancellor Abraham Diaz Gonzalez. Within one meeting the council had succeeded in alienating the entire faculty, inflaming the students, and widening the struggle to include the protection of the curriculum reforms Diaz had tried to institute.

War overtook the campus. Rock throwing battles between right- and left-wing students rivaled those of European and Mexican universities. Classes became arenas for debate which degenerated into fights. The cafeteria was physically split along status orientation lines. Each side had its hang-out and woe to the opponent who wandered onto that turf.

The government continued to bungle the situation, sending its police on campus to support the armed campus guards, and that provocation, in a country where the university is traditionally sacrosanct, won more *independentista* supporters. "Soon, we had no problem bringing out thousands to our actions," Fupista commented. "By 1968 or so, I would say that everyone who opposed the draft believed in independence."

The fight against the ROTC would continue at that feverish pitch until the early 1970s, as the war and the draft wound down. It yielded several incidents which are now part of the independence movement's folklore.

In 1970, the students voted overwhelmingly in a referendum to dump ROTC. That referendum was held shortly after another pitched battle on the campus. Pro-independence students had marched on the ROTC and members of the Socialist League, a small independence organization confronted the ROTC students in their barracks. The ROTC responded predictably with gunfire and some of the *independentistas* were ready and armed for their comeback. Riot squad police were called onto the campus which was promptly closed.

At the end of the 1970 academic year, it was obvious that nothing would be done about the referendum and the ROTC would stay. The reaction of students was clear in about half the student body's refusal to accept their diplomas from then Chancellor Jaime Benitez. At one point, during the ceremony, student Carmen Noelia Lopez slapped the chancellor in the face.

The student movement created during those two years of explosive protest is significant for two reasons. First, it has remained active, closing the university periodically and keeping the issues within the public realm. For example, the last strike at the University, in 1981, was for all practical purposes a failure: the leadership was expelled and the administration refused to capitulate to the curriculum demands put forward. But the *independentistas* who led that strike were in the media and the public attention almost constantly, and that exposure enabled them to address major political issues before a very wide audience.

Secondly, the student movement has served as a kind of reservoir of leadership talent, the arena where working-class men and women acquire the political knowledge, organizational skills, and the experience of confrontation which has proven key in the development of movement leaders. This assumption of leadership by former university students has been a natural and logical process. Many of these activists were victims of purges which forced them out of school before graduation and into industrial jobs—jobs that meant union membership and a level of activism that naturally goes with such employment.

Meanwhile, and perhaps more importantly, the Puerto Rican working class is changing like the working classes of many industrial and post-industrial economies. With the island's economy shifting to a service economy and with the bloating of public sector employment to its current grotesque proportions, the professionals—engineers, accountants, planners, and teachers—are forced to work in the mass-production conditions that were once typical only for industrial employees. In some cases, like teachers, these professionals have formed labor unions that are among the island's most militant; in others, the hint of incipient organizing is increasingly present.

The simple fact is that not only have working-class youngsters become the majority of the university's student body but university graduates have become a substantial percentage of the island's working class.

Labor Movement

Despite a high level of student involvement, the labor movement has its own independent dynamic and has been an arena of significant struggles.

The sweeping changes brought by the industrialization of the island in the 1950s changed the labor movement dramatically. The worker in the cane fields became a worker on the factory line, responding to a different schedule and set of conditions. The countryside was increasingly abandoned for the city. And government, which had been a small, colonial affair at best was transformed into a massive industry.

The building of the infrastructure to nurture this industrialization required armies of on-site workers, planners, clerical, and administrative personnel and many of those same workers were needed to keep that structure running. Before 1950, for example, the Transportation Department had 320 full-time employees. Ten years later, its payroll was over 3500 and today it's twice that. The same is true of the municipal bus system and the fire department.[11] In 1959, the government published an advertisement encouraging "any man who can drive a car" to learn how to drive a bus or large truck. "The training took about three days," Juan Cintron, a veteran bus-driver in Rio Piedras remembered. "You learned the route you were to drive, you learned something about the vehicle and the regulations and off you went. That's how badly bus-drivers were needed."

As the PNP's Ferre came to power, the economic situation was deteriorating and workers were feeling a need for some kind of protection. The island's traditional labor movement, true to its now acquiescent character, had largely ignored the smaller shops created by Operation Bootstrap. Like the Seafarers International Union which stayed on the docks and the ships where full employment was almost guaranteed by the constant shipping needed in colonial territory, the labor movement made no effort to recruit the new labor force to its ranks. So when the need for large unions was greatest, the large unions weren't where they were needed. In 1968, when Ferre took power, only 12 percent of the island's labor force was organized by a recognized union. The time was ripe for an explosion and it occurred that year with a Teamsters' strike (over wages and working conditions) which crippled portions of industry. That strike lasted two months, covering newspaper front pages with news of its intense militance and violence, and polarizing labor leaders into those who supported it and those who remained quiet.

The epoch of labor peace was over.

In Puerto Rico, there was already a group of young labor leaders whose interest lay in the organization of workers. Some had spent time in the turbulent university; some were simply young workers who were tired of their conditions. Reacting to the obvious vacuum, these new leaders began organizing and the results were immediate. In 1969, a two month strike closed the General Electric plant in the Rio Piedras area; a new union, the Workers' Guild was formed and won representation. In 1969, two construction strikes were the scenes of bloody battles between workers and scabs and another new union, the National Union, developed from those struggles. For the first time since 1940, a scab was killed.

In 1970, bus drivers, demanding representational rights for a new union, went on national strike. Transportation was crippled in the major cities; publicity abounded. In that same year, electrical workers struck in two cities, also forming a national union of their own. The next year, Teamsters struck again and firefighters voted in a new, island-wide union. In 1975, the island's telephone workers began a strike which crippled the island's phone system and became symbolic of labor power.

In the years between 1969 and 1975, Puerto Rico was hit by nearly 100 strikes—more than a dozen of national impact—and most of those strikers founded new unions.

The rash of strikes gave the labor movement of Puerto Rico a major boost, transforming it from an often polarized movement (of bureaucratized organizations on the one hand and immature, albeit more democratic and militant, groups on the other) to a dynamic political force. Workers had become a vocal, feisty presence in the political arena.

It also made impossible a repetition of the easy economic transformation which the *Populares* had performed twenty years before. As the Puerto Rican economy was rapidly shifting into

more concentrated, specific, and larger industries which required
fewer workers, the small labor unions acted as a kind of brake on
precipitous closings and work force cuts. They didn't stop the
economic retrenchment but they mitigated it and made it more
difficult.

Most of these unions average a few hundred workers each,
based in one or two workplaces. There are several larger formations. While American labor is dominated by the massive machinery of the modern labor union, whose finances and structure rival
those of the bosses they rarely strike against, Puerto Rico's
movement is made up of small, flexible unions, capable of igniting
strikes at any time.

Besides those characteristics, the militant unions had in
common a wariness toward AFL-CIO dominance on the island, a
fierce jealousy of their organizational independence, and, for the
most part, leadership that is a good deal to the left of labor leaders
of the 1950s. In 1971, forty of these unions, including some of the
most active and largest, formed a United Workers' Movement
(MOU) which remained vital as a coordinator of inter-union support for the entire decade.

The MOU also began labor support of May Day activities,
sometimes drawing thousands of workers into these socialist
sponsored marches. The MOU coordinator in 1975, Pedro Grant,
one of Puerto Rico's most respected labor leaders, said, "It's folly to
say that these are pro-independence unions. Perhaps some of the
best leaders are *independentistas* and socialists but the members
are not, for the most part, consciously revolutionary. That's not to
say, though, that their actions are not pro-independence."[12]

Just what strikes do to strikers' consciousness about status is
impossible to ascertain. But post-strike polls after the telephone
and electrical strikes have shown that, for a time at least, independence gained support as an alternative. For example, after a
three month long electrical workers' strike in 1978, a poll on status
thinking was taken. Workers were asked which party served their
interests best. During the strike, of course, the principle foe of the
union had been the governing PNP, the statehood party, and
logically, the poll showed no support for them. The PPD received
about 35 percent of the votes. The rest of the votes, a full 65 percent,
were won by the two independence parties. Clearly, the labor
struggle had promoted opposition, not just in the workplace, but in
the political sphere as well.

Yet, with all the success, colonialism has presented the labor
movement with a perplexing problem—the professionalization of

the island's working class. Not only are the teachers and social workers facing mass production conditions that cry out for organization but even lawyers and doctors are now finding it virtually impossible to enter the entrepreneurial mini-world of private practice. More and more—as is true in the United States—medical and law school graduates are moving into large institutional work, often as alienating and routinized as the construction of an automobile. And the trend of proletarianization has arrived hand in hand with its cousin—unemployment—giving rise to groups like the national organization of unemployed physicians currently operating in Puerto Rico.

What does the labor movement do about the consistent growth of this sector within the working class? While there have been several noteworthy attempts to organize professional associations and committees within these sectors, union organizers have been consistently unable to move in because of the laws curtailing the labor organizing of civil service workers. Automatically, because of those laws, the labor movement cannot reach over 35 percent of the working population and, as the ranks of highly-trained workers grow (and the ranks of industrial and private sector workers shrink), the labor movement finds itself condemned to organizing a disappearing population.

Certainly, this is one explanation for the virulent resistance of both PNP and PPD leaders to changing the civil service laws on union organizing and it is the principal reason why this issue has remained among the most important for both the labor movement and the independence movement.

The Arts

In Latin America, students, workers, and artists have traditionally produced radical movements' leadership and, to a great extent, their ideology. Puerto Rico is no exception. Indeed, in Puerto Rico, pro-independence thought so thoroughly dominates the arts that one is hard-put to find Puerto Rican artists who don't at least "intellectually" support independence.

Like movement activists in general, these artists don't play a uniform role in Puerto Rican life. Some artists produce work that is infused with political sentiment and ideology. This is certainly true of many of the poets, painters (like master Lorenzo Homan), and those involved in theater. For others, art is a means of exploring and discovering the Puerto Rican reality, subtly inserting into

the artistic idiom a vision that is specifically working-class. All of
it is, of course, vital and it makes the arts one of the most important
arenas of political struggle on the island.

This assertion is frequently contradicted by activists' allu-
sions to the "colonization of culture," but Puerto Rican popular art
is among the most vital and provocative areas of Puerto Rican
daily life. At the very least, the contradictions within colonialism
and the battles provoked by those contradictions are all well
reflected within Puerto Rican arts.

For example, most Puerto Rican access to the arts comes
through television; 80 percent of Puerto Rican families have one.
And Puerto Rico's television is a bastardized version of the "wasteland" critics in this country often speak of. The few island-
produced variety and comedy shows are surrounded by American
situation comedies whose characters make jokes in a dubbed
Spanish that renders the humor meaningless or by an endless
cycle of action series in which dialogue is unimportant. Not only is
the result mind-dulling but it condemns Puerto Ricans to entertainment based on a reality that is not even close to their own, just
exacerbating the problem of low self-esteem.

Yet within this wasteland there are spots of lucidity, power,
and quality. For decades now, local comedy shows have used
working-class humor to explore situations and problems—like
alcoholism, loss of job, and the marginalization of young people.
Such seriousness of purpose has bled into other popular artistic
forms. For if Jacobo Morales's 1986 feature-length film *Radamas y
los Demas*—a comedy of manners about successful Puerto Ricans—
represents one of the first serious film projects made specifically by
Puerto Ricans, the innovative and intellectually provocative
music of people like Danny Rivera, Lucecita Benitez, and Haci-
endo Punto en Otro Son—to say nothing of explicitly political
singers like Roy Brown—has been around since the 1960s. All of
these people are *independentistas*.

What's especially admirable about these expressions is that
they endure in the face of enormous obstacles. Colonial power
doesn't take lightly to its critics and, although such expressions
are constitutionally protected, they are certainly not financially
supported. The money in Puerto Rico is in the night-clubs and,
since these mostly cater to tourism, it's easier for many of these
singers to book television appearances than it is to get bookings in
the clubs.

The poets and fiction writers of Puerto Rico face that problem
in an even more exaggerated way. Except for a few small enter-

prises ("One guy working his head off in his garage," as Pedro Juan Soto put it), Puerto Rico has no major publishing house. You either publish your work yourself, get a Latin American house interested, or languish in an unread state.

"What is amazing," Soto said, "is that so many poets and short story writers do publish anyway. They work to get the money and, like some kind of craftsman, they put their own material out." There are exceptions; Soto is one as is Gonzalez and Luis Raphael Sanchez, whose stunning novel *La Guaracha de Macho Camacho* is an island success and has been published in English to excellent reviews. But there are dozens of superb writers who haven't been circulated outside of the small group of loyal readers receiving their self-published work.

In a sense, this lack of opportunity exposes colonialism for these writers and can only deepen their already present anti-colonialist vision. For it is difficult to think of one major fiction writer or poet who is not an *independentista*. In the vicious circle of colonialism, their oppositional voices go unheard; they are kept out of circulation.

What is most refreshing about this literature is that it's based, like indigenous television, on working-class experience and has been for decades. Jose Luis Gonzalez and the "fifties generation" writers (who actually came to prominence in the late 1960s) managed to inject into Puerto Rican literature an unprecedentedly serious description of working-class life. It's difficult, at this point in history, to understand the enormous change this signified. Up to then, little literature even admitted the existence of working-class life; these writers made it their entire focus.

Additionally, this "proletarian" approach to literature permitted these writers to treat Puerto Ricans in the United States as part of the Puerto Rican experience. Soto's *Spics* is distinguished not only by the simple power of its portraits of Puerto Ricans in this country but by the very fact that such an eminent writer chose to write about these people *as Puerto Ricans*.

Soto himself explained this in an interview when he said, "Once you understand our people as the people who work for a living, who face everything that this implies, you have to pay attention to the Puerto Ricans in the United States. Because one of the things workers faced in Puerto Rico was having to move to New York." Indeed, the very concept of a New York Puerto Rican is one of Puerto Rican art's greatest achievements. To incorporate an immigrant people as part of the Puerto Rican experience is to cut into the reality of colonialism. No longer is the trip to New York a

severing of ties with the island, as many islanders believed, nor is
it a kind of failure on the part of the island's people to hold on to
their own. It is now viewed by all these writers as a central aspect
of the modern Puerto Rican existence, a perspective that leads to
an almost automatic indictment of colonialism.

The Puerto Rican artists of the fifties generation sought to
bring the reader into the Puerto Rican home for the first time.
There, contrary to popular conception, the woman emerges as a
dynamic figure—a presence that provides strength and intelligence. Not that these are entirely enlightened visions, as Acosta
Belen points out, they are "women under men's authority...often
the reason for the tragedies which face the men."[13]

There are advances, however. In Rene Marques's play, "La
Carreta" ("the Oxcart"), one of Puerto Rican literature's master-
pieces, women are portrayed as having the strength of character
and will that was necessary to keep families together during the
early portion of Operation Bootstrap when poeple were migrating
from the countryside to cities and finally to New York.

A Legacy of Repression

The summer sun wipes out nights quickly in Puerto Rico and
by 6:00 a.m. on August 30, 1986 it was already shining. So the
small army of men in commando uniforms walking down a
residential street in Rio Piedras with automatic weapons in hand
probably had no problem finding Coqui Santaliz's apartment.

Santaliz, a reporter for the English-language *San Juan Star*,
had just risen when about twelve of the men broke her door down,
held her at gunpoint, and started the nightmare that would last all
day.

When they finally left late that afternoon, the commandos
had ransacked the house—seizing manuscripts of a novel and a
book of poetry, notebooks, and tapes of interviews and music. They
spent a dozen hours in the house, occasionally intimidating
Santaliz, constantly asking her questions and, all the time,
refusing to produce more than their credentials. But the credentials spoke eloquently, identifying the commandos as agents of the
FBI.

While the events at Ms. Santaliz's house were taking place,
other commandos were doing the same things at the houses and
offices of some thirty-seven other people. As military helicopters
hovered in support, the agents held people in their homes for as

long as eighteen hours, sometimes physically abusing them.

They took reams of notes, tapes, film, and mountains of books from several lawyers, writers, and scholars. They wrecked dozens of original celigraphs of the reknowned painter Antonio Martorell. And they ransacked the offices of *Pensamiento Critico*, a respected journal of critical thought, confiscating notes, tapes, film, typesetting equipment, and the rollers of the printing press.

Eleven people were arrested and taken to Hartford, Connecticut where they are currently being held.

As the dust settled, word about the raids spread, and a virtual sonic boom of protest exploded. Things became somewhat clearer. First of all, the raids were obviously aimed at the island's independence movement—all the homes and offices belonged to *independentistas*. Secondly, the FBI had trained for this type of action in Puerto Rico; their raids were skillfully conducted and coordinated. Finally, the FBI is ready to face serious protests and they are prepared to violate both the U.S. and Puerto Rican constitutions in dozens of ways if necessary.

Federal officials say they were looking for a man who allegedly robbed a Wells Fargo truck in Hartford, Connecticut two years ago. Government officials say the man, Nelson Gerena, is part of a clandestine organization called *Los Macheteros* which has taken credit for several fairly spectacular attacks against military installations in Puerto Rico.

The eleven people arrested by the FBI and brought to Hartford are being charged with some link to the Wells Fargo heist. The government isn't saying what the connections are or what evidence it has. The eleven claim, through their lawyers, that there are no such links and that the government has no case.

There are many questions being raised about those arrests and even New York area FBI officials (who reporters consider the most cynical in the agency) privately express doubts about the case. "Maybe a few of those guys are real suspects," said one official who works on surveillance of Cuban exiles, "but it seems like a pretty motley crew and besides, do you really need all those people to plan to lift some money off a truck? I think we may see a few charges dropped."

Even more baffling is the government's explanation of the raids on those not arrested. "You have to remember there were two simultaneous investigations going on," the U.S. Attorney in Puerto Rico said. "There was the Hartford investigation and one going on down here." The only concrete statement of intent on that second investigation was made by Attorney General Edwin Meese right after the raids. "We are sending a message to terrorists," he said, "that their bloody acts will not be tolerated."[14]

The statement was greeted in Puerto Rican newspapers with something approaching ridicule. What, several columnists asked, can you blow up with the typesetting equipment and printing press of a magazine or with Santaliz's music tapes? And why these thirty homes, owned by a cross-section of island professionals whose political viewpoints—while all pro-independence—vary from Marxist to social democrat?

For many, the implication is obvious. "This was a frontal attack against an entire movement and an entire set of ideals," said Ruben Berrios, president of the social democratic Puerto Rican Independence Party and a man who has traditionally been low-key in his statements. "It is virtually an act of war upon our people's will, determination and rights."[15]

The FBI is, of course, no stranger to the Puerto Rican independence movement. As Freedom of Information Act files indicate, for twenty years at least, the FBI carried on one of the most intense campaigns of harassment and repression in its own history. And the campaign was directed not simply at discrediting the movement but effectively destroying it.

It was a campaign characterized by misinformation, surveillance, telephone harassment, purposeful misrouting and opening of mail, physical attacks, and even possible murder. At times the campaign was carried on by the U.S. intelligence agencies, at times by the Puerto Rican police with FBI knowledge. This history of "dirty tricks" proves that the United States government—contrary to its oft-repeated protestations—is not a disinterested and impartial observer, but a key and vicious player in the struggle over the island's status.

Mr. Hoover's Memo

In August of 1960, J. Edgar Hoover sent a memo to the FBI's San Juan office:

> The Bureau appreciates that the situation in Puerto Rico is unique because of conditions in Cuba, its accessibility to Puerto Rico and the seemingly unrestrained travel of some of your subjects to Cuba...Puerto Rican subjects who have frequently travelled to Cuba are primarily concerned with seeking independence for Puerto Rico... [T]he more positive effort must be made not only to curtail but to disrupt the activities of the Puerto Rican nationalists."

It must be kept in mind that this memo was sent before Cuba declared itself socialist, shortly after the fall of Batista. The memo implies some ongoing FBI activity prior to this moment, although no evidence is published in the documents to prove that.

During the next year, Hoover became more concerned. A 1961 memo worries that, "A small core of nationalists advocating Puerto Rican independence [has grown] into a movement of considerable magnitude wherein communism has a greater part than even in the past..."

The file of Cointelpro documents finally made public contains massive deletions of whole sections and cross outs on every page. The cynic might say that the worst has been extracted but what remains still boggles the imagination.

Rather than summarize each of Hoover's memos to San Juan, the ones which order some action and the ones which congratulate the office on having carried it out, it might be best to simply outline and categorize the basic methods...all of which are contained and described in detail in the FBI memos.

1) *Intelligence activities.* For eleven years, the FBI courted, paid, and worked with informants who would report on virtually every movement meeting, including most of the internal matters in the various parties and organizations. The memos provide a disturbingly clear picture of the internal discussions that took place during the formation of the Puerto Rican Socialist Party, for example.

The FBI kept telephone surveillance on both the PSP and the PIP for virtually the whole eleven years. Why this was done was not even made clear. Both were legal organizations, working above ground, whose leaders had never been convicted of any crime or even minor infraction. They had never been linked in any serious way—short of the frenzied accusations of some reporters and statehooders—to any of the many bombings and other violent activities going on. They were public opposition movements.

PSP leader Juan Mari Bras was watched, for more than five years, on a twenty-four hour basis. At one point, Hoover chastized his operatives for not "looking hard enough for something being done."

Thousands of photographs and tape recordings were made of independence advocates. One memo details a conversation between a PSP organizer and someone in the main office about an upcoming demonstration. The listener admits to being bored.

2) *Harrassment*. Dozens of memos describe activities of harrassment. An operative put together a newsletter, to be distributed on campus, detailing the sexual misadventures and financial shenanigans of independence leaders. "The misinformation campaign," says the memo, "has achieved some success."

Hoover urged his men to send their informants to meetings with some expanded responsibilities. "Questions and issues could be raised to waste time, disrupt meetings and make their ongoing work more difficult."

The FBI in San Juan began a campaign, attributed to the Puerto Rican Socialist Party, which criticized and made fun of Puerto Rican Socialist League leader Juan Antonio Corretjer, often considered the island's greatest poet. The two organizations fought over the campaign and shots were fired. No one was killed, said the report, but "the impact was highly fruitful."

3) *Forgeries*. Where newsletters and leaflets weren't helpful, stolen checks and false bank balances were used. In 1968, the FBI attempted to withdraw hundreds of dollars of funds from one MPI account under the name of another independence leader. The bank resisted the withdrawal letter, however, and the report called the attempt unsuccessful.

4) *Physical violence*. The memos list more than fifteen reports of agents and informants physically disrupting meetings, starting fights, attacking demonstrations... all gleefully self-congratulatory.

At times, the direct action was in the form of direct attribution. In 1967, for example, the FBI published a series of "findings" submitted in public letters by Hoover himself.

The letters stated that the *independentistas* talked of independence but, "will actually have as their purpose the furthering of the aims of communism in Latin America." This crude redbaiting, totally illegal for the FBI, took place before the 1967 plebiscite on status. Similar memos, during election periods, reflect a similar content.

At times, those points of view were channeled through media "friends." Several memos report that island newspapers, like *El Mundo*, have accepted FBI written editorials for their editorial pages. About fifteen memos speak of "successful operations" by "loyal media personnel."

There are memos about FBI written letters seeking to have honest *independentistas* expelled from organizations as agents, memos about false information naming people as informants submitted surrepticiously to the organizations, memos which detail campaigns to discredit organizations (at one point issuing openly racist leaflets over the signature of the MPI and other independence groups), and there are memos about the creation, by the FBI, of right-wing groups on campus and in various towns to combat independence ideas and even disrupt the activities of the movement.

That is what is contained in the published material. It is but one volume out of hundreds. There are seventy-five volumes, a few of which are published, about *independentista* Mari Bras alone. "They reflect the general activity of the FBI toward the movement," he told the U.N. "But some of the memos are dated 1976 and 1977; long after Cointelpro was ended as an FBI activity.

"At one point, there is a detailed description of the death of my son, in 1976, at the hands of a gun-toting assassin. The bottom of the memo is fully deleted leaving one wondering who the assassin was. The main point, however, is that the memo is almost joyful about the impact this death will undoubtedly have on me in my Gubernatorial campaign, as the head of our party, in 1976."[16]

There are also several memos from San Juan reporting on Mari Bras's two heart attacks with recommendations as to how the pressure on the leader could be compounded to force more of the same. One memo even states: "It is hardly idle boasting to say that at least some of the Bureau's activities have provoked the situation of Mari Bras."

Although this last could be the chest beating of an agent whose careerism and *machismo* had become rather perverse, it does reflect the mentality of the FBI. Independence was an enemy, not something to be watched for criminal activity, but something to be combatted, disrupted, and beaten.

The government says it quit its surveillance and disruption of the independence movement in 1971 and there is one memo to that effect. Whatever horrors were there in the rest of those hundreds of volumes are things of the past, says the FBI. This assertion, however, is contradicted by the study group which presented its stunning findings drawn from the documents to the UN in 1978. They claim, "There is substantial evidence to show that, though the name no longer is used, the actions continue." In 1976, for example, a sworn deposition by a union leader in the Ponce area claimed that the FBI was right in the middle of the cement workers' strikes, which were a major catalyst for the increased militance of the labor movement.

Security Associates (one of the top strikebreaking firms in this country), paid dozens of citizens to attempt to destroy that strike by driving trucks into the plant. Though this is an obvious unfair labor practice, what was truly illegal was that the firm attempted to get the workers to shoot strikebreakers and plant bombs. Two weeks after the meetings, at which the workers refused the request, bombs exploded and the leadership of the union was arrested, by the FBI for the bombings. The arrests, although making the strike difficult, never even came to indictment.

The FBI obviously worked overtime on the independence movement but it got more than a little help from its friends. Over the last six or seven years, the Puerto Rican police have become so embroiled in publicly exposed repression against the movement that, today, hardly anyone is surprised at new revelations.

There is substantial evidence of guilt by commission and omission.

The omission is highlighted by the fact that, over the last fifteen years, 170 attacks—beatings, shootings, and bombings of independence organizations and activists—have been documented. The offices of the pro-independence newspaper *Claridad* have been bombed three times; its printing press has been bombed twice and burned once. There have been four shootings, none fatal, at those two buildings. The PIP's offices have been bombed three times. The PSP's bombed once; Mari Bras's home was burned down once. There have been countless attacks and beatings of people at rallies and pickets, to say nothing of "unsolved" incidents of beatings of *independentistas* walking the streets. These are routine. The 1975 bombing of a rally in Mayaguez that killed two restaurant workers was more dramatic, but like the other 170 attacks, remains unsolved. Although many right-wing organizations claimed credit for nearly seventy of these attacks, not one person has ever been arrested or brought to trial.

Not to say the police have been inactive: there have been an almost equal number of trials of all types against *independentistas* and here, the other side of the coin functions: not one has been convicted.

Most of the top leadership of the PSP has, at one time or another, been indicted for some bombing or other "subversive activity." All cases were thrown out for lack of evidence, except the arrest of two members in a home which was allegedly a bomb factory; no explosives were recovered, and the case was eventually overturned.

One of the most recent and famous cases, which did go to jury, was that of Miguel Cabrera, a Teamster organizer. At the very best, his case profiles how policy works in Puerto Rico. In 1976, Cabrera had been spearheading the Teamsters' drive for new membership. Puerto Rican Teamsters share with their U.S. counterparts the reputation for punching their way through walls, if necessary, to win organizing drives. Cabrera, a soft spoken, often smiling giant of a man, was no exception.

In September 1977, during the height of the Teamsters' organizing drive, a U.S. lawyer named Allen Randall was shot to death. A "workers' commando" took credit for the killing, presenting two documents which detailed Randall's activities. Randall had been the legal counsel to the National Labor Relations Board during the period when that board outlawed the militant National Union Construction Firm. (Two of its leaders, by the way, were indicted for killing a strikebreaker—another case which ended in acquittal.) As legal counsel to some of the top firms operating in Puerto Rico—firms that specialized in using law to obstruct worker organizing—Randall was the epitome of the corporate militant.

Two days after the killing, the police identified Teamster Cabrera and several other organizers as the culprits. Cabrera told the police to come to arrest him if they had any evidence. It took them three months. Cabrera was shocked, "This surprises even me."

The evidence produced in January of 1978 was Cabrera's fingerprint on the *second* of the Workers' Commando communiques. This evidence had surfaced, they said, in October, a week after police said his fingerprint was on the *first* communique. The evidence became known as "the hopping fingerprint."

While the print hopped, another bizarre twist was added to the story. Juan Caballero, a Teamster shop steward, disappeared. Cabrera was arrested by police and the suddenly materializing FBI in January of 1978. He was prevented from organizing the entire year and a half until his trial in 1979.

The union could do little to bring Cabrera back, but its leadership was profoundly disturbed by the disappearance of the disciplined Caballero. They investigated and found witnesses who had seen Caballero at police headquarters shortly before his death.

Island-wide outcry alleging the torture of Caballero began and, two weeks later, on October 25, 1977 police produced a body they said was found in El Yunque rain forest. It had been there for about ten days, was badly decomposed and bound by electrical wire.

The Teamsters went wild, accusing the police of killing Caballero. The police countered: Caballero had been a suspect in the

Randall killing and probably had been killed by associates afraid he would talk.

The whole thing became even more bizarre when the body's dental structure did not match those in Caballero's medical records and a bone fracture in Caballero's right hand didn't show up in x-rays of the corpse.

Police explained that fingerprints were the evidence they had used for identification. And where were the prints? They had cut off the fingers of the one good, undecayed hand of the corpse to match them with Caballero's records. When the defense counsel in the Cabrera case asked for the fingers the police explained they had been lost.

The allegations that police had kidnapped Caballero and killed him during a torture/interrogation session and then disposed of the body continue to this day. They have never been proved, of course.

During Cabrera's trial a major witness was produced. Angel Hernandez Tanco told the jury, after delaying his testimony for a week, that he was offered money to kill Randall by one co-defendant, Culberto Cordero (an offer he said he refused) and was told, after Randall's death, by co-defendant Luis Parilla, that the Teamsters had Randall killed.

Hernandez Tanco was an admitted professional assassin who had been serving an eight-year jail sentence (the product of another government "star witness" deal) for murdering four people and wounding two others. He'd gotten around, having been the star witness in four government trials. "The man has really participated in a lot of murders," one journalist wrote. Allegedly a drug addict, Hernandez Tanco's contradictory testimony was ripped to shreds by the defense.

The hopping fingerprint, which ended up finally on the second communique, was blasted as well. It seems the FBI had requested Cabrera's fingerprint a day before they received any of the other evidence, including the communiques, leaving the question dangling: What were they matching the print to?

The defense hardly presented a case or a summation. The prosecution had hung itself. In his closing statement the prosecutor said the fingerprint did not indicate guilt but perhaps it meant there was some kind of conspiracy. He also said Charles Manson and Mafia figures had been implicated by hired killers whose evidence the juries in those cases had accepted.

This jury was different. They ignored a second summation given by the prosecution after the defense spent five minutes summing up. Prosecutor Pestanan Segovia literally ranted about Teamster-Mafia connections and the terrorism that was ripping the island apart. The jury returned not guilty verdicts in three hours. Said jury foreman Antonio Fuentes: "It was an easy decision... [T]here was really a lot of talk and evidence but absolutely nothing showing the defendants guilty."

The lingering question of Caballero's disappearance is overshadowed by the question of what the FBI's participation was in the affair. There is no doubt about the impact: it halted the Teamsters' drive at a crucial period and forced the union into a defensive posture. This type of case can be recounted dozens of times: key people tried at key moments and removed from leadership positions by evidence that suddenly falls apart at trial.

It is difficult to pin all of this on the FBI, however, because the published documents end with the disbanding of Cointelpro in 1971.

It is known that FBI personnel met with police prior to the assassination of two *independentistas*, in an ambush in the Cerro Maravilla area in 1978. According to the police, the two were on their way to bomb a police station and were accompanied by a police informant who admits having planned and urged the bombing. A *carro publico* driver who witnessed the ambush testified that some three police who were waiting in the bushes shot without giving orders of any kind and without either of the youngsters raising their own revolvers. "It was a planned murder," he told a commission set up to investigate, "and it was carried out like that."

This commission returned findings sharply critical of the governor, but, not surprisingly, the governor took no action. The Justice Department also investigated and found no wrongdoing. And the electorate apparently eschewed this laissez-faire approach to what remains among the most scandalous incidents of police brutality in modern Puerto Rican history. The Cerro Maravilla incident became a central issue in the 1984 elections, the symbolic shorthand of a PPD campaign based entirely on the New Progressive Party's corruption and white-wash of police activities. Hernandez Colon's campaign grouped, under the term "Cerro Maravilla," police brutality, police involvement in illegal drug distribution, and other crimes as well as what the PPD claimed was "a deepening incompetence" on the part of the police administration.

Upon his victory, the PPD's Hernandez Colon quickly proceeded to effectively dismantle much of the metropolitan police hierarchy and threw his support behind a civil lawsuit brought in federal court by the families of the victims. In March 1987, that lawsuit was settled for an award of $1.3 million, the largest in the history of Puerto Rico.

"The point of all this [evidence of repression] is not to say the FBI has played dirty tricks," Mari Bras told the UN in 1977. "Everyone admits that. Nor do we express surprise that this repressive activity continues. The real point is that the evidence soundly disproves the allegations by the United States government that it has not been involved in the status debate, that it is an objective force. For twenty years, and actually since the beginning of the American presence, it has manipulated public opinion and fought actively against independence."

The Challenge

No one can underestimate the effect of this repressive campaign on the independence movement and its ability to attract popular support. Yet, no *independentista* can use this repression as an explanation of the current state of affairs or as an answer to the lingering question all *independentistas* face: Why is Puerto Rico still a colony?

It is a universally accepted truth that the independence leaders are among the most respected leaders on the island. Indeed, no political movement can boast the popular respect this movement enjoys—for the average Puerto Rican, the image of an *independentista* is synonymous with integrity, commitment, and intelligence. Additionally, the issue itself is a winner. For the average Puerto Rican, saying "I'd like to see my country free" is almost a given; it is the universal reaction to the status question.

Independence is a solution of enormous emotional resonance advanced by a movement which enjoys tremendous respect at a moment when conditions make it objectively clear that nothing else will work. So why isn't Puerto Rico independent or, better expressed, why aren't most Puerto Ricans *independentistas*? Part of the answer to that question can be found in Frantz Fanon's *The Wretched of the Earth* where the author explains that independence movements too often blame colonialism for colonialism's continued existence.

The problem is that the independence movement has proven incapable of taking an obviously popular and logical desire—the desire to be free—and convincing the Puerto Rican people that they can, in fact, achieve that goal and protect it.

While there are many explanations for that failure, it is clear that the majority of Puerto Ricans don't share with their *independentista* compatriots the confidence that the island can win its independence and build a society that will remain independent. As vital and powerful as the movement continues to be, it is chronically plagued by that failure—condemned to being a movement of opposition, of moments of convincing criticism. It is a movement that demands attention when it criticizes but is largely ignored when it poses its alternative. To an extent, this is a perfectly understandable response to what have been fundamentally unpalatable alternatives put forward by the independence movement thus far.

The problem is best illustrated through the island's two most important pro-independence organizations of the last decade—the social democratic Puerto Rican Independence Party (PSP) and the Marxist Puerto Rican Socialist Party (PSP). It is important to look briefly at the arguments of both formations because, throughout the tumultuous 1970s, they were the independence movement's most influential forces—massive, visible, and intensely active.

In both cases, there were serious flaws in political perspective that almost destroyed both groups, rendering them mere shells of their past popularity. In the PIP's case, their political program was based on the expectation that a consensus would not materialize on its own. They believed independence was a status that was completely logical; thus, the U.S. government would eventually see the light; the Puerto Rican electorate would see the light; and independence would win in an election and be granted by the Congress. Not that the PIP's strategy should be caricatured as groping for a Fabian-like agreement based on enlightenment: the PIP believed in pressure, demonstrations, and denunciations. For example, in a 1978 press conference at the U.N., Berrios explained that "American tax-payers are subsidizing a country and not benefitting from it. When the American people realize this, as they currently are, they will demand independence. In Puerto Rico, the people of the island are quickly understanding how important independence is...They know they can't continue with the current situation, so they are quickly coming into our movement."[17] One must, of course, take into account the political leaders license to "overstate" the case. Indeed, Berrios would have been irresponsible to tell reporters that his party doesn't stand a chance of winning its struggle. But the content of that statement, which stands four-square on the PIP program, goes beyond the bounds of optimism. American tax-payers are simply not going to begin clamoring for Puerto Rico's independence because they are subsidizing it; taxation has never been the spark for any anti-imperialist activity with the exception of the American revolution and, then, North America was a colony.

Additionally, while people were joining the independence movement, they weren't doing it at quite the rate the PIP estimated. Indeed, two years after Berrios made that statement, the PNP was re-elected. If anything, the crisis was driving people in the other direction.

This sense of over-expectation is even more apparent in the recent history of the other electoral party, the Puerto Rican Socialist Party. A formation which arose in the early 1970s from the Pro-Independence Movement (MPI), that party was the island's principal Marxist formation during the 1970s.

The MPI, founded in 1959, was an organization which combined the more militant *independentistas*, including former nationalists, with a new group of Marxists. Its perspective, frequently described as the "New Struggle," was based on the concept of a "colonial crisis" in Puerto Rico. The crisis, the theory held, would bring mass movements and a rush to *independentista* thinking among the populace.

When the MPI converted itself into what it defined as a "revolutionary party of the working class," it dropped that slogan. But the expectation of colonial crisis as a kind of revolutionary panacea remained. For the PSP, the revolution seemed to be always around the corner, as close as the increasingly acute colonial crisis. And while the PSP stopped publicly using the colonial crisis theory shortly after its creation, it seems to have been unable to grow beyond it theoretically and practically. It is with the insight, "the colonial crisis has come," that the PSP leaders and analysts have proven the island's most perceptive. But rather than deliver the masses, particularly the working class, to pro-independence thinking, the crisis has merely shifted much of that sector to the statehood party.

Organizationally, as every ex-PSP member will quickly attest, the flaw had a staggering impact on the party. The politics of crisis produced an atmosphere of tension, of imminient explosion that translated into a nearly frenzied activism. It strained resources, kept the PSP's tight-knit organization in a state of constant tension, and made burn-out into a problem of epidemic proportions. Certainly, those organizational tensions led to the PSP's eventual splintering at the end of the decade. But the principal problem wasn't organizational, it was political.

While the idea that this colonial crisis would accelerate the liberation process actually fueled PSP members with an enthusiasm unmatched within Puerto Rican politics, it also eventually led to frustration. Things were obviously degenerating in Puerto Rico much more rapidly than the movement was growing. And while the PSP continued to explain to people how Puerto Rico was facing imminent chaos, the Puerto Rican people didn't seem to agree. Certainly, most of the population believed things were getting worse but the impact of Puerto Rico's problems on people was mitigated by the fact that social degeneration in Puerto Rico was gradual and not perceptible on a daily basis.

That, of course, is the entire independence movement's problem. It is not so much that the independence alternative is not supported but that the question of status simply is not the foremost issue on people's minds. The movement has yet to make the possibility of a non-colonial alternative part of the popular Puerto Rican consciousness. The severe fragmentation within the PSP, which has driven off most of its membership, has forced an examination of this very question within the independence movement—particularly its large socialist component. Dozens of smaller groups, mostly former PSP members, have produced documents, public debates, and prolonged discussions about the strategic implications involved and each seems to have its own answer. History shows that these questions are resolved over time and in action; concrete work is ideology's litmus test. If there is one true answer, one successful strategy, it isn't clear yet.

Still, no one can deny that both the PIP and the PSP had an enormous impact on Puerto Rican politics during the 1970s and that that impact can still be felt. The popular acceptance of the independence movement as a legitimate political force, the respect it has won, the attention it demands when its leaders take positions, and the growing cynicism among Puerto Ricans about their government—fueled by both the conditions in the country and the movement's denunciation of them—remain a significant part of Puerto Rican political culture. Besides, Puerto Rico's past makes clear that periods of organizational disarray in the independence movement are only moments, short pauses really, in the history of what has proven to be a powerful and resilient movement.

7

Conclusion

Dangerous Opportunities

In 1944, when young Luis Muñoz Marin told his Senate colleagues that independence was the only real solution to Puerto Rico's problems, a debate raged over possible, untried status alternatives. Advocates of independence, autonomy, and assimilation could argue their choices with impunity and without the burden of a track record.

That, of course, is no longer the case. The fact that Puerto Rico has been considered a Commonwealth for nearly forty years and has been governed by both the PPD and its pro-statehood rival, the PNP, has dramatically changed the way politicians debate island status and the strategies their electoral parties employ. Today, political debate among the two colonial parties is an exercise in responsibility-dodging and the reason for that is best exemplified by Doña Licha herself.

I spent one afternoon and two mornings speaking with Leticia Roman in 1975. I had never seen her before and have not seen her or heard from her since. She is only one of the thousands of people I have interviewed during nearly twenty years as a working journalist and her comments on those three days have never before found their way into print. When I began working on this book, I came across my notes from those conversations and was convinced that this had to be her book.

It was not that she reflected the people of Puerto Rico; no one person could capture so complex a nation. Nor did she share my personal perspective on what road the country should follow; Licha was a PPD supporter. For me, Puerto Rico is Licha's island because her life so clearly personalized the impact of colonialism.

I remember speaking to her as she stood in her sandals cleaning fish, occasionally glancing at the water as if to assure herself it was still there, telling time by the water, pinpointing where the fish would bite that day, and predicting the weather by the waves, currents, and winds. Water was a part of her, and she was a part of the precise, timeless ecosystem which has supplied Puerto Rico's fish, dictated its climate, molded its environment, and served as its link to the rest of the world. That ecosystem, like Leticia herself, is rapidly becoming an anachronism.

Puerto Rican populism proved Faustian in character, having made a pact which brought it political ascendancy but traded away the island's future. Now colonialism is entrenched more deeply than ever and Puerto Rico faces a future of possible social and political degeneration, ending in its destruction as a nation.

After decades of government by advocates of Commonwealth and advocates of statehood, it has become increasingly obvious that colonialism is a house with a rotten structure; it cannot be redesigned, nor can it hide its deterioration. The U.S. economic expansion of the 1950s, which bolstered Operation Bootstrap and hid its flaws, has run its course. The mystique and excitement accompanying the massive structural changes brought by Operation Bootstrap, like the shift from agriculture to industry, are no longer possible. The silky garments of Populist opportunism have been ripped off. A real change must take place and, because colonialism cannot make such a change itself, the island is in perpetual crisis.

In Chinese, the word for "crisis" is roughly "dangerous opportunity." Never has the moment been so opportune for the Puerto Rican independence movement—the only movement which advocates a clear alternative to what is becoming an unbearable situation.

The opportunity brings with it several challenges, not the least of which is to come to grips with the fact that independence itself is not necessarily an answer. Political independence is a status enjoyed by almost all the countries in the world, including countries where people starve, are brutally repressed, live desperate lives, and are still under neo-colonial control. Independence in a country like Puerto Rico cannot be painted on like a brush stroke; it must be accompanied by major changes in the structure of the island's social and economic life. Even those necessary changes provide no guarantees. The reconstruction of a country is a tumultuous, painful process and here too, examples abound of well-intentioned, initially optimistic revolutions, which have failed.

Despite the crisis, those who believe these changes must come have yet to convince the majority of Puerto Rico's people. And so Puerto Rico's crisis affects not only its colonial system but the movement that would replace it.

The Logical Choice

The situation is complicated by an ironic fact—for *independentistas*, independent status seems so logical and obvious that there has been a great temptation not to think or talk much about what an independent Puerto Rico would actually be like. In fact, it has proven much easier over the years to merely denounce colonialism and describe its alternative as vaguely as possible.

No one has challenged the *independentistas* to describe their vision of the future. Independence is so powerful an alternative that its opponents do not really argue against it; they attack its proponents or evade the question.

Statehooders argue that independence is impossible, that Puerto Rico is too small, that it must be dependent on the United States to survive. This is, of course, patently absurd. Dependence on the United States is the island's problem, not a solution and independence does not imply isolation. Indeed, in today's interdependent world, isolation would be impossible. There is a huge difference between healthy reliance among countries and dependence, a result not of size, but of development.

The *Populares'* stance is even more opportunist and illogical. For the most part, PPD officials simply insist that Puerto Ricans do not want to be independent, and they pull out voting statistics as proof. The *Populares* are hiding behind the political iron curtain that blocks the flow of real political debate—the institutionalized patronage system, the millions of dollars expended on campaigns, the sheer weight of U.S. economic and political

presence on the island, and the inferiority complex that results
from centuries of colonial life. What is truly surprising is that,
despite these obstacles to real political debate, an estimated 20
percent of the electorate voted for one of the pro-independence
candidates in 1980.

For decades, *independentistas* have wasted their time debating both the PNP and PPD, neither of which make plausible
arguments against independence. The real problem independence
advocates face is that the majority of Puerto Ricans are not
sufficiently confident that they will survive in an independent
country. The most important question for *independentistas* to
address is the viability of their plan.

Not long ago, the most prominent *independentista* theory was
that the degeneration of Puerto Rico would automatically force
people to realize that colonialism was bankrupt and unbearable
and would move people to embrace independence as a solution. It
hasn't happened. The crisis of colonialism has deepened but active
participation in the independence movement has not. Indeed, the
independence movement of today—while still sizeable and
active—has been reduced over the past five years to dozens of
fragments, its principal parties severely divided and its organizations in disarray, functioning without a coherent theory or
strategy. And so the question for today's movement is not so much
how it debates the other parties, but how it will put forward its own
realistic alternative—one that will capture and win the confidence
of the people.

Any attempt to provide a solution to this problem in this book
would be inappropriate and ultimately fruitless. Strategy develops
collectively among many people, over a period of time filled with
practical work, lessons, and intense discussion. Still, it can be
safely said that, at this point, the independence movement
remains an opposition movement rather than a liberation movement and the most obvious proof of that is the demographic
character of the movement itself.

Of the People and Apart from Them

It is particularly frustrating to independence activists that
Puerto Rico's majority rejects their politics while embracing their
activism. The average Puerto Rican speaks of this movement with

enormous respect. Its activists are admired for their courage, commitment, and integrity, its leaders for their intelligence and honesty. In the eyes of many Puerto Ricans, the independence movement embodies the finest qualities of leadership and political involvement, much like the Nationalist Party did for the masses of people in its day. For example, the independence movement is often approached for support by workers on strike. Also, like Nationalists, it is not representative of the very Puerto Rican working class that so highly respects it. If that problem was important during the Nationalist heyday, it is even more critical in an industrialized, urbanized Puerto Rico where the only class capable of truly changing the society is the working class.

The independence movement has, for most of its recent history, been led by professionals, with an astounding preponderance of lawyers. Even the growth in pro-independence sentiment and movement involvement among labor leaders since 1970 has not really transformed the class background of the movement's leadership. In the case of the pro-independence parties and left-wing organizations, working-class leaders have played a uniformly small role.

Such leadership demographics are logical. The movement's resurgence in the early 1960s was based primarily on the campus struggles of that period and it was out of those struggles that the leadership developed. The MPI developed out of a small group of former Nationalists and student leaders, with a sprinkling of ex-members of the island's Communist Party. The PIP was never, nor did it ever pretend to be, anything but an electoral formation directed by progressive politicians and professionals. The same is true of particular "issue oriented" organizations and movements.

As a result, the island's working class—particularly its unionized workers—remains decidedly to the right of its professional and student populations. The movement consequently remains isolated from the people who would convert its oppositionist character into that of a genuine liberation movement. Such isolation impacts not only on the culture of the movement—the way it communicates and organizes, the subtleties of attitude and approach difficult to describe but perceptible in action—but, more importantly, the movement's very policies and perspectives.

The Colonial Crisis

Just how the composition of a movement affects its politics is dramatized by independentism's continuing confidence in the colonial crisis as a revolutionary panacea. While this approach affects different organizations in different ways, it has affected the entire movement by making the development of a comprehensive strategy unimportant and even unpalatable to many leading organizations.

Although one group of *independentistas*—the Marxists—have put forward a theory of liberation, it has not been adopted by the movement as a whole. Indeed, one of the problems with many Puerto Rican Marxists is that they advance the notion that a strategy is something developed by only one party or organization within a wider movement—sort of a secret hidden agenda or master plan that the amorphous, unsophisticated mass movement would not understand. Such elitism is hardly useful in a country like Puerto Rico where full participation of a large majority will be needed to bring about national liberation. Every successful liberation movement in the past has had a shared, clearly delineated strategy; that is what separates it from a mere movement of opposition.

There is no such strategy in Puerto Rico. Not only is there no real consensus among different independence organizations as to what types of struggles are to be organized and how resources are to be shared among the different tendencies, but there has never been consensus about what the movement concretely wants. Does it seek to transform society? Does it seek to share power? Does it envision an armed conflict, an electoral campaign? Certainly, this lack of unity is a measure of movement immaturity because such strategies will emerge as the struggle intensifies. But it is just as certain that the movement has never undertaken a serious internal discussion of these matters and this lapse is rooted in the movement's hyperbolic reading of the objective situation in the country: the "colonial crisis." Not only is it considered acceptable to be passive about strategy and planning (the objective conditions make qualitative change imminent), but it even becomes relevant to ask, "Why bother with unity at all?" In many instances, the struggle has degenerated into a race to see which party or organization will be best placed to catch these masses of people falling from the tree of unenlightenment onto the pastures of pro-independence sentiment.

Such thinking is arrogant and anti-historical. There have been far too many cases in which crisis has driven the working class, not to the left, but to the right. And, to an extent, this exact dynamic is unfolding in Puerto Rico, evidenced by the substantial support most industrial workers give the PNP.

Revolution by Diplomacy

The one place where the entire movement did often get together organizationally and strategically was in its recruitment of "international support." The fact that Puerto Rican independence is supported by the Movement of Non-Aligned Nations and by the United Nations De-Colonization Committee, that it has been specifically taken up by international conferences in virtually every continent, and that it is a publicly proclaimed position of nearly fifty of the world's governments is tribute to the success of this work.

Most impressive of all, the movement has attracted support for a struggle that is nowhere near as developed and popular as, say, the Vietnam or Nicaraguan struggles were. What got these organizations to risk their political chips on a struggle that was obviously underdeveloped compared to others in the world?

Convincing the world to take this step was a difficult and demanding job for pro-independence organizations who managed to get together and hammer out common positions and approaches before each of these conferences and before the yearly UN discussions. It is not merely coincidental that the only place in which the PIP's Berrios and the PSP's Mari Bras appeared together since 1974 was at the UN—the grudging unity of the leaders of these two rival organizations was instrumental in getting results. It is also a grating affront to many third world nations that the United States maintains a colony in Latin America. Working so feverishly for international support, however, is symptomatic of the movement's very problem: its dependence on the idea that colonialism will soon collapse of its own accord.

This poor reading of reality has not only affected the movement as a whole, it has proven fatal to some of the movement's organizations. Nowhere is this more evident than in the spectacular disintegration of the Puerto Rican Socialist Party.

During the 1970s, the PSP was the movement's acknowledged left-wing leadership; even its critics agree that it was the movement's largest, best organized, most active, and most visible force. In the late 1970s, the PSP was wracked by a series of internal disputes which left it badly splintered and without its most experienced and capable leadership—a small organization which manages to publish its newspaper and engage in a few activities. The crowning blow was symbolized by a public, acrimonious debate—replete with ugly charges and counter-charges and the virtual wholesale resignation of its membership, including its legendary leader, Juan Mari Bras.

The whole tragic affair has spawned a library's worth of published analyses, some thoughtful and provocative, some useless and vituperative. The differences among analysts are profound and the bitterness is understandable. Yet, most people involved in the break-up of the PSP seem to agree on one thing: life in the PSP was a frenzied existence of constant tension and endless activity. To the PSP, it seemed, each new policy or major action by the government represented a major threat to the island's future; every development brought the collapse of colonialism closer; every demonstration or campaign showed incomparable growth in pro-independence and even pro-socialist sentiment. It was the same "colonial crisis" perspective in new, more sophisticated clothing.

Clearly, if crisis is the key to independence and independence is right around the corner, then militants should work tirelessly, much like marathon runners, summoning up the "kick" during the last half-mile. The only problem was that, after a decade it became increasingly obvious to PSP members that the race was still very far from over. The PSP just ran out of steam, collapsing in a recriminatory, disillusioned, fragmented heap.

Not much time is spent here on the PSP's collapse because the past demonstrates that these crises in the movement are momentary. Besides, the PSP and the era it represents in *independentista* history affected Puerto Rico profoundly and positively in ways that will be felt for a very long time. Among other things, it redefined the *independentista* approach, helped build the movement by recruiting people in unprecedented numbers, and stopped the colonial government from completing many plans which would, in fact, have damaged the island's future. The PSP of the 1970s was, on balance, an enormous success. Perhaps most significantly, however, its demise provided one great benefit:

independentistas no longer believe that independence is just around the corner.

The Three Clichés

The independence movement will undoubtedly revive itself in a more organized fashion, armed with the realization that its principal responsibility is to develop a strategy designed to move the Puerto Rican people to win their independence. In developing that strategy over the next period, the movement will face another difficult challenge: it must continue to answer, not the tired clichés of the PNP and PPD activists, but the very real concerns of the people themselves.

Although the PSP once published a comprehensive program which described an independent, socialist Puerto Rico in impressive detail, the larger independence movement never unified around that document or that vision. A movement that seeks to change Puerto Rico must have some clarity about what will replace the *status quo*.

Sometime, somehow, the independence movement must define certain points of unity that it can present as absolutes to its people—a kind of popular contract which can be the basis of recruitment to the movement, the *independentista* version of Muñoz Marin's rhetorical "give me your vote now and take it back if I fail you." Such a contract would demonstrate to the Puerto Rican people that the movement is truly sensitive to them and willing to make such concerns the centerpiece of its approach. There is much debate about what such a program should contain, but it is not within the scope of this book to elaborate on it. There are, however, three issues that must be addressed if independentism is to be at all successful in making its voice heard.

The Non-Isolationist Economy

Modern day independentism views the goal it advocates through the prism of the contemporary world and reaches the simple and reasonable conclusion that, to survive, Puerto Rico must exercise consummate control of its own economy. This means, for most independence supporters, not just the legal power to prevent the plundering investment so typical of contemporary neo-colonialism but the ability to structure an economy that can simultaneously use and replenish its resources to meet the fundamental needs of its population and to encourage the expansion of those needs. In other words, real development means not only allowing a certain quality of life but actually leading people to expect and work for a higher quality of life.

Such social and economic development cannot emerge from the anarchy so prevalent during Operation Bootstrap; at this time, on this island, development requires a controlled and planned economy and the intelligent balance between two areas of production—production geared to survival and production geared to growth. Looking at an economy that way is somewhat jarring since capitalist economies, and many socialist economies, have traditionally divided production into agriculture and industry. For an economy like Puerto Rico's, that makes little sense. Meeting basic needs in Puerto Rico is no longer the sole province of agriculture, animal-rearing, or fishing—the traditional food economies. The society is now at a point where technology has become a given and housing, cars, and even certain basic electronic equipment (like televisions) must be considered basic needs. Their production or acquisition (if they are produced elsewhere) must be a priority.

Failing to make them a priority would mean opening the economy to dependence. For example, with virtually every household in Puerto Rico owning a television set, an uncontrolled dependence on foreign countries for such goods would damage the economy's independence. That's not to say that Puerto Rico must produce all consumer goods—clearly trade is called for—but it must plan their purchase intelligently.

On the other hand, some food industries are also growth-oriented. For example, agriculture and fishing could easily develop to the point of providing the island with important international credits from other countries seeking that same production. If the Dominican Republic can sell its agricultural production throughout Latin America, why not Puerto Rico?

All of these questions raise a major economic issue: the need to open Puerto Rico to international trade. The economy of an independent Puerto Rico would have to be based at least partly on the needs of other countries, particularly those Latin American countries with whom trade would be easiest and most intense.

Some economists call this type of economic planning "credit accumulation"—a kind of international barter in which Puerto Rico might, for example, make certain products available in exchange for others produced abroad.

A balanced economy capable of using industrial and natural resources to meet people's needs through direct provision or trade makes sense. Indeed, it's the only way Puerto Rico could survive. But the idea that such an industrial program could be immediately (or even quickly) put into effect is folly. One of colonialism's most salient features is the compartmentalization of industry that renders much industrial and technological equipment absolutely useless to a small, independent country. Pharmaceutical plants in Puerto Rico cannot just be acquired and used by the country because they produce, at best, a small portion of the final, marketable product.

Sobering as that reality is, an independent Puerto Rico would have to reorganize its economy both structurally and physically, transforming not only the way production is planned and oriented but where and how it was carried out, and the places where that happens. In short, industry must be rebuilt.

While freely admitting that this, of course, will be an arduous and protracted process (an admission that has too seldom been made by the movement), *independentistas* must commit themselves to doing what colonialism has never permitted the island: trading with the international community.

Pluralistic and Open Democracy

There are few examples of democratic government in the recent history of Latin America. The region's political legacy of repression, underdevelopment, and dictatorship combined with the powerful, paranoid, anti-communist rhetoric that flows throughout the American continent leaves Puerto Ricans almost immobilized in their fear of change and political upheaval. Fear of right-wing dictatorship in Puerto Rico is easily matched by the "communist" threat imposed from abroad, a dynamic that Governor Hernandez Colon used to exploit in the mid-1970s when he would privately refer to the PSP's Mari Bras as "our Cuban ambassador." The political consciousness of this Latin America island again suffers from its colonial relationship with the United

States because it reflects much of the entrenched jingoism prominent among U.S. right-wingers.

Wedded to their electoral system—patterned as it is after that
of the United States—many Puerto Ricans believe that they enjoy
political stability and fundamental constitutional protections
that many Latin American countries do not. It is a theme
constantly sounded in the United States by politicians and
government leaders, a mechanistic mysticism that entirely ignores the social and economic underpinnings of stability and
upheaval. And it is made even more credible by the constant
instability that characterizes the political situation in the rest of
the hemisphere. Unfortunately, when many Puerto Ricans see the
virulent repression in Chile, for example, and the abuses suffered
by the Misquito Indians in Nicaragua, they see the same thing.
Nearly a century of propaganda has made them ill-equipped to
differentiate between a rotten regime with no future at all and a
young revolutionary government that is sometimes overly rigid
and arrogant but that is trying to open a path to the future.

The result of all this is that Puerto Rico is today so entrenched
in the idea of a constitutional system and electoral democracy that
the quality of most people's lives is overlooked. In fact, it was not
stubborn unemployment, the stagnating economy, or the other
social problems facing the island that toppled the government of
Carlos Romero Barcelo in 1984; it was the public perception of his
involvement in the police cover-up of the Cerro Maravilla killings.

What's more, for Puerto Ricans, democracy has a very specific
structural definition. It is synonymous with plurality and the
constitutional guarantees of political expression, organization,
and mobilization which nourish such plurality. While Puerto
Rican popular thinking vacillates constantly, Puerto Ricans
would never support a political system which does not guarantee
rights that have been part of the island's political culture for
almost a century. In and of itself, the right to freely talk about
problems does not imply the opportunity to solve them and an
independent Puerto Rico would have to expand upon this limited
form of democracy to ensure the participation of all sectors and the
full empowerment of all people. But anything less than what
currently exists would never be palatable.

An Independent Foreign Policy

"How do we know," many people ask, "that we won't be overrun by some larger country when we are no longer protected by the United States?" The clearest answer is that, rather than being protected, we have already been overrun. That response, however, evades the real feeling of powerlessness fostered by centuries of colonialism and the fear spawned by an almost complete ignorance of the world outside the island's borders.

It is difficult to explain to those who have never experienced Puerto Rico firsthand how a developed country so close to the United States can be so isolated from the world. It is instructive to remember that Puerto Rico trades with no one but the United States and has little contact with the international community. Consequently, people don't have the sense that Puerto Rico is part of an international community or that it could count on certain protections were it to achieve independence.

Joining the international community as an independent nation, Puerto Rico must maintain an independent foreign policy. Puerto Rico would have to be neutral, and from the beginning, would have to avoid aligning itself intimately with any one country or group of countries. It must be stressed that, once independent (even if enormous hostility accompanies that victory), Puerto Rico would aggressively seek dignified and mutually respectful relations with the United States.

Is such a position conceivable in a hemisphere where independence is, at best, a precarious way of life for small countries? Recent history shows that, when faced with a prodigal neo-colony, Washington is vengeful and hostile. Furthermore, the impulse to attack true independence is not unique to conservatives. If the policy of Ronald Reagan toward Nicaragua—so often maligned by North American liberals—has been relentlessly war-like and sadistic, the policy toward Cuba started by the liberals' patron saint, John Kennedy (and carried on by his successor Lyndon Johnson), is a model of subversion, isolation, and both indirect and direct attack. The conservatives' policy toward Nicaragua has included constant military attack (for example, the mining of a harbor) and a variety of grotesque "covert activities," but the liberals also have a legacy of sabotage, subterfuge, and even the attempted assassination of Cuban President Castro.

In this context, can anyone legitimately condemn Cuba or, to a lesser extent, Nicaragua for turning to the Soviet Union for both

economic and domestic aid? And, given that aid, can anyone be
surprised that Soviet influence has grown in both those countries?
No condemnation is levelled here nor surprise expressed. There
would be no Cuba or Nicaragua as we know them today without
Soviet aid. Owing a country your life does tend to increase its
influence. Contrary to what North American officials say, Soviet
activities in this hemisphere have been, on balance, not a threat to
the hemisphere but a contribution to its future.

Still, that is not the whole story; the world is not pure. As Fidel
Castro pointed out at the Cuban Conference on Energy in December, 1984: "Our dependence on our Soviet comrades has been key to
our survival and detrimental to our development...If we want to
stop being junior partners in the international community, we
must begin paying our share, shouldering our economic burden,
and producing for ourselves."[1] Cuba's spectacular economic debt
to the Soviet Union remains that country's most difficult long-
range economic problem and is an example of something that is to
be avoided by all other countries seeking their independence.

So the question becomes how Puerto Rico can avoid such
strangling dependence and survive.

The answer, ironically, is that it can avoid dependence by
concentrating on its own survival, by vigorously pursuing a
balanced and independent economy, and by vigorously defending
a democratic political structure. Such a statement is deceptively
simple, of course, because developing an independent economy
and maintaining political autonomy will be difficult. Even so,
these tasks will be further hindered by the threat of a U.S.
invasion—an eventuality which the recent history of Grenada
proves very real. There are factors that mitigate that possibility
somewhat—Cuba's existence is one and the presence of two
million Puerto Ricans in this country is another. But, if the United
States decides that there is no alternative and that it is politically
palatable, it *can* invade. Preventing that is partly a matter of the
new government's tactical approach. Nicaragua is certainly an
excellent example of how tactics can hold off a direct invasion.

In the end, this problem will probably take care of itself. If the
Puerto Rican people decided to be independent from the United
States, they will do so and the threat of invasion will not deter
them. The challenge for the independence movement is to convince its people that it will fiercely defend its country's independence and exercise an independence that will demonstrate that
commitment.

These brief comments on three areas—economy, internal

democracy, and foreign policy—do not even remotely qualify as a description of an independent Puerto Rico. But an independence that excludes any of these three points could never really address the problem of colonialism, nor could it win the kind of popular involvement that would give it the right to challenge colonialism.

Disappearing Solutions

Who can say when Puerto Rico will be free? At the moment, independence doesn't look imminent but political conditions can change rapidly. The key for the independence movement is to be patient, to understand that a mature liberation movement seizes opportunities and stretches the possibilities but it can never do more than that. Time and the social forces at work each day must be allowed to proceed and political movements must understand that they play only one role in a very complex and dynamic drama. That the independence movement has begun to understand itself that way is cause for rejoicing.

The patience with which the independence movement now views Puerto Rico's future, however, must be tempered by the appreciation of a sobering, even disturbing fact. Contrary to the thinking prominent in the 1960s that "time is on our side," time is actually running out.

Each day, the economy of Puerto Rico loses more of the few vestiges of indigenous initiative left as small local businesses are forced to close. Each day, agriculture comes closer to complete disappearance. Each day, the environment becomes more and more hostile to any productive use of land or water. Each day, public debt and private debt grow; military presence grows; the electoral road-show becomes more and more ludicrous; the social ills of crime, alcoholism, addictive behavior, and insanity become more common; and the country's best minds leave.

Colonialism does not just exist, it actively destroys the colony, making independence less and less feasible and making people less and less willing to seek it. Independence is not just a solution. It is the only means to survival and, when all is said and done, it is the most important point on the agenda for Doña Licha's island.

Footnotes

Chapter Two

1. Brau, Salvador. *Historia de Puerto Rico*, (Editorial Coqui: Rio Piedras, 1966) p.9.

2. *Ibid.*, p. 10.

3. Letter, Ponce de Leon, original at Museo Nacional, Madrid, Spain.

4. Wagneheim, Kal. *Puerto Rico: A Profile*, (Praeger Publishers: New York, 1970) p. 42.

5. *Ibid.*

6. Rivera Quintero, Marcia. "Incorporacion de las Mujeres al Mercado de Trabajo en el Desarrollo del Capitalismo." Essay contained in *La Mujer en la Sociedad Puertorriquena*, (CEREP: San Juan, Puerto Rico, 1980) p. 43.

7. Maldonado-Denis, Manuel. *Puerto Rico: Una Interpretacion Historico-Social*, (Editorial Siglo Veintiuno: Mexico City, 1970) p. 23.

8. Lewis, Gordon. *Puerto Rico: Freedom and Power in the Caribbean*, (Monthly Review Press: New York, 1963. Updated edition, Harper Torchbooks: New York, 1968) p. 29.

9. *Ibid.*

10. *Ibid.*, p. 41.
11. Flinter, George. *An Account of the Present State of the Island of Porto Rico*, (Layman Press: London, 1934) Work cited by Lewis, *op. cit.*
12. Rivera Quintero, in Belen, *op. cit.*, p. 42.
13. *Ibid.*, p. 44.
14. Abbad y Lasierra, Frey Inigo. *Hisotrica Grafica, Civil y Natural de la Isla de San Juan Bautista de Puerto*, (Ediciones UPR: Rio Piedras, 1959).
15. Brau, *op cit.*, p. 14.
16. Cruz Monclova, Lidio. *Historia de Puerto Rico*, (Editorial Universitaria: Rio Piedras, 1970) p. 904.
17. Lewis, *op. cit.*, p. 31.
18. *Ibid.*
19. Cruz Monclova. *op. cit.*, pp. 42, 43.
20. Betances leaflet cited in Wagenheim, Kal and Olga Jimenez. *The Puerto Ricans*, (Anchorage Books: New York, 1973) pp. 77-78.
21. Maldonado-Denis, *op. cit.*, p. 46.
22. Maldonado-Denis, *op. cit.*, p. 39.
23. Lewis, *op. cit.*, p. 35.
24. Wagenheim, *Puerto Rico: A Profile, op. cit.*, p. 63.
25. As quoted in Wagenheim, *Ibid.*, p. 63.

Chapter Three

1. Interview with Luis Munoz Marin. Summer, 1977.
2. This increase in the sugar content of foods has been documented in dozens of popular works. Yet, the seminal work continues to be William Duffy's *Sugar Blues*. (Warner Books: New York, 1975).
3. Capetillo, Luisa. As quoted in Quintero Rivera, A.G., *El Movimento Obrero en Puerto Rico*, (CEREP: Rio Piedras, 1974) p. 41.
4. *Ibid.*

5. Igleisias Pantin, Santiago. Speech to the Delegates Assembly of the Free Federation, 1918. Original can be found in University of Puerto Rico's Library.
6. Rivera Quintero, in Belen, *op cit*, p. 57.
7. Marcano, Juan. "Paginas Rojas," 1914. Selected sections found in University of Puerto Rico's library.

8. Munoz interview, *op. cit.*

9. NACLA (North American Congress on Latin America) Report on the Americas, 1983. [Need article name and author]

10. Lewis, *op cit.*, p. 114.

11. Quote generally attributed.

12. Hamilton, Charles. Lecture, Columbia University. Spring, 1983.

13. Perloff, Harvey. *Puerto Rico's Economic Future: A Study in Planned Development* (University of Chicago Press: Chicago, 1949).

14. Munoz interview, *op. cit.*

15. *Ibid.*

16. *Ibid.*

17. Berrios, Ruben. Speech to the United Nations Committee of 24. New York, 1977.

18. Eisenhower, Dwight David. As quoted in Associated Press dispatch.

19. Albizu Cam,pos, Pedro. Speech at Lares, Sept. 30, 1950. Primary print source Babin, Maria Teresa and Steiner, Stan Borinquen, *An Anthology of Puerto Rican Literature*, (Vintage Books, 1974). Speech was recored and can be heard on the record "Habla Albizu Campos," (Paredon Records: New York, 1972).

20. Corretjer, Juan Antonio. Speech at Guaynabo, 1965, reproduced in *Albizu Campos*, (Siglo Ilustrado: Montevidedo, Uruguay, 1974).

21. Jordan, Robert. As quoted in the *Herald Tribune*. March 14, 1952. p. 17.

22. Rivera Quintero, *op. cit.*, p. 97.

23. Albizu Campos, Pedro. Article on can strike in Quintero Rivera, *op. cit.*, p. 102.

24. Speech in 1954, various sources including *El Imparcial* and Associated Press.

25. Lewis, *op. cit.*, p. 237.

26. Tumin, Melvin M. with Feldman, Arnold S., *Social Class and Social Change in Puerto Rico*, (Bobbs Merrill: New York, 1971).

27. Conversation with the author.

28. Rodriquez, Helen. Speech in 1975. (Reprinted by Committee to End Sterilization Abuse: New York).

29. *Ibid.*

30. Kelly interview reprinted by CESA.

31. *Ibid.*

32. Badillo, Americo, "Bread, Land and Liberty," *NACLA Report on the Americas,* March/April, 1981.

33. *Ibid.*

34. Planning Board of Puerto Rico, statistical study. Published by Economic Development Administration, Puerto Rico. 1975.

35. American Petroleum Institute, "Report on Domestic Petroleum." (Washington, 1979).

36. University of Puerto Rico Study Group. "The Puerto Rican Economy," (Rio Piedras, 1975), unpublished paper.

37. Paul Horowitz, "Puerto Rico's Pharmaceutical Fix," *NACLA,* March/April, 1981.

38. Economic Development Administration, Annual Report. (Puerto Rico, 1977).

39. *Wall Street Journal,* Sept. 20, 1980.

40. Horowitz, *op. cit.*

41. *Wall Street Journal, op. cit.*

42. Cripps, Louise. *The Case for Puerto Rican Independence* (Alfred Schenckman: Cambridge, Mass. 1970). p. 78.

Chapter 4

1. Horowitz, *op. cit.*

2. University of Puerto Rico Study Group, unpublished survey of Puerto Rican economic conditions, 1982.

3. Economic Development Administration of Puerto Rico, *Annual Report),* 1983.

4. Interview with various reporters, including author. Washington, 1974.

5. "The Food Stamp Scandal" was originally broadcast on the program "Sixty Minutes," CBS, 1977.

6. Fox Piven, Frances and Cloward, Richard. *Regulating the Poor,* (Vintage Books: New York, 1972).

7. Garcia, Neftali, Lecture, San Juan, 1974.

8. Environmental Protection Agency. Report, 1976.

9. Statistical study, not intended for publication. Puerto Rican Department of Health (Rio Piedras, 1978).

10. *Claridad,* June 11, 1975. p. 3.

11. Interview by phone.

12. Interview by phone, 1978.

13. *New York Times,* April, 1976.

14. Garcia, *op. cit.*

15. Buckley, William, syndicated column, April, 1980.

16. Environmental Protection Agency, "Report on Territorial Waters," testimony before Interior Committee. 1978.

17. Garcia, conference, San Juan, 1975.

18. Government of Puerto Rico, Department of Tourism, *Report*, 1983.

19. Maldonado Denis, Manuel. Lecture, Queens College. New York, 1973.

20. *Annual Report to the Legislature*, Deptartment of Justice, Puerto Rico, 1981.

21. Author interview.

22. Fernandez-Mendez, Eugenio. Paper presented at Hunter College conference on Puerto Rican studies, 1971.

23. Arbona, Remarks during conference, New York, 1976.

24. Interview by author.

25. World Health Ogranization, "Annual Statistical Abstract and Report on Work." Sections on U.S. and Territories, 1982.

26. Interview by the author.

27. Deptartment of Health, Puerto Rico, *op. cit.*

28. *Ibid.*

29. *Ibid.*

30. Mari Bras, Juan, "Comentario Politico." *Claridad*, March, 1979.

31. Bureau of the Census, U.S. Department of Labor. "The 1980 Census: An Abstract on Puerto Rico," (Washington, 1983.)

32. Bonilla, Frank and Campos, Ricardo. "A Wealth of Poor: Puerto Rico in the New Economic Order," *Daedulus*, Spring, 1981.

Chapter Five

1. Senior, Clarence *Puerto Ricans: Strangers then Neighbors* (Quadrangle Books: Chicago, 1965).

2. Gonzalez, Jose Luis. *Cuadernos Sobre La Cultura,* (The Center for Puerto Rican Studies: New York, 1974).

3. Interview with reporters.

4. Bureau of Labor Statistics, U.S. Deptartment of Labor. *Puerto Ricans in the United States*, (New York, 1983).

5. Budget Report to the Legislature of Puerto Rico, 1983. The Commonwealth of Puerto Rico.

6. Bureau of the Census, "The 1980 Census of Population: Statistical Abstract," New York.

7. Municipal Government of Camden. Population survey not intended for publication, 1976.

8. Census Bureau, *op. cit.*

9. U.S. Council on Civil Rights. Report of Findings.

10. Bureau of the Census, *op. cit.*

11. Bureau of Labor Statistics, *Monthly Report* (March, 1983).

12. New York State Human Rights Commission, hearings on situation of Puerto Ricans, (Albany, 1970).

13. Author interview.

14. Gonzalez, Jose Luis. "The Passage" in Babin, Maria Teresa and Steiner, Stan, *Borinquen: An Anthology of Puerto Rican Literature*, (Vintage Books: New York, 1974).

15. Address to annual convention of the Congreso Boricua by Executive Enrique Arroyo. Trenton, 1982.

16. Author interview. New York Parks Department.

17. Gerena Valentin, Gilberto. Speech before the Puerto Rican Congress, 1981.

18. Data provided by American and Eastern airlines in interviews by the author.

19. New York Board of Education statistics, 1979, obtained by author.

20. *Ibid.*

21. Fuentes, Luis. Speech at Manhattan College. Bronx, New York, 1970.

22. Blaut, James. "Are Puerto Ricans a National Minority?" published in *Monthly Review*, (New York, May 1977.)

23. New York Catholic Archdiocese, statistics, compiled 1982, unpublished.

24. Interview by the author.

25. Center for Puerto Rican Studies, *op. cit.*

26. *Cuadernos sobre la cultura*, (Center for Puerto Rican Studies: New York, 1974).

27. Blaut, *op. cit.*

28. Maldonado Denis, Manuel. *Puerto Rico: A Socio-Historic Interpretation, op. cit.* Epilogue to first English edition.

29. Blaut, *op. cit.*

30. *Daily News*, June 12, 1976. p. 15.

31. Carmichael, Stokely and Hamilton, Charles. *Black Power: The Politics of Liberation*, (Random House: New York, 1967).

32. Nixon interview. *New York Times*, (April 22, 1973).

33. Allen, Robert. *Black Awakening in Capitalist America*, (Doubleday Anchor: New York, 1970).

34. Velez, Ramon. Interview by author, 1968.

35. Conversation with author.

36. Ortiz, Hildemar. Statement during 1971 conference, Hunter College.

37. Badillo, Herman. Interview by author, 1978.

Chapter Six

1. Morales Carrion, Arturo. *New York Times,* August 12, 1984.

2. Romero Barcelo, Carlos. speech in San Juan, 1976.

3. Romero Barcelo, Carlos. Television interview, PBS, New York, 1977.

4. Lopez, Franklin Delano. Interview in *El Dia*, February 19, 1979.

5. Romero Barcelo, Carlos. *Newsweek*, 1977.

6. Colberg, Severo. Statement to Congressional hearings on the Carribbean initiative. As reported by Associated Press, 1983.

7. Amoco Tourist Guide to the Carribbean, 1983. Amoco Corporation, Houston, Texas.

8. Hernandez Agosto, Miguel. Speech to United Nations Committee, 1977.

9. Ferre Luis, speech. 1968.

10. Maldonado Denis, Manuel. Conference at University of Puerto Rico, 1973.

11.

12. Grant, Pedro. Speech at Harlem Fight Back. New York, Oct., 1974.

13. Acosta Belen, Edna. "Ideologia e Imagenes de la Mujer en la Literatura Puertorriquena Contemporanea" in *La Mujer en La Sociedad Puertorriquena* (CEREP: Rio Piedras, 1980) p. 125.

14. Meese, Edwin. Meet the Press, May, 1982. NBC, New York.

15. Berrios, Ruben. Press Conference, 1978.

16. Mari Bras, Juan. Speech before United Nations Committee of 24. Sept., 1977.

17. Berrios. Remarks made during press conference at UN, 1976.

Chapter Seven

1. Closing Remarks to National Conference on Energy. Havana, Cuba, December 1984. Taken from Cuban telecast.